I Will Tell of

My War Story

A Pictorial Account

of the Nez Perce War

Cash Book

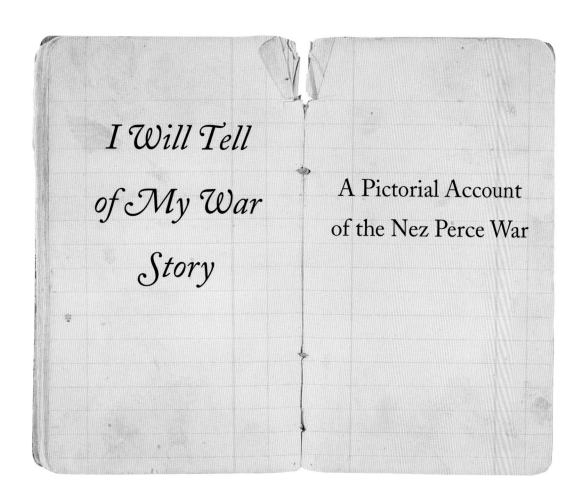

I Will Tell
of My War
Story

A Pictorial Account
of the Nez Perce War

SCOTT M. THOMPSON

A Samuel and Althea Stroum Book

UNIVERSITY OF WASHINGTON PRESS *Seattle & London*

in association with

THE IDAHO STATE HISTORICAL SOCIETY *Boise*

*This book is published with the assistance of a grant
from the Stroum Book Fund,
established through the generosity of
Samuel and Althea Stroum.*

Copyright © 2000 by the University of Washington Press
Designed by Veronica Seyd
Printed in Hong Kong

LIBRARY OF CONGRESS CATALOGING-IN-PUBLICATION DATA

Thompson, Scott M.
    I will tell of my war story : a pictorial account of the Nez
    Perce War / Scott M. Thompson.
      p. cm. — (A Samuel and Althea Stroum book)
  Includes bibliographical references.
  ISBN 0-295-97943-7 (alk. paper)
    1. Nez Perce Indians—Wars, 1877—Pictorial works.
      I. Title. II. Series.
E83.877.T56 2000
973.8'3—dc21   00-021609

page ii: Calfskin cover of the Beck-Warner *Cash Book*

Contents

Preface

Far left: Henry Eneas was photographed wearing clothing typical of that worn by warriors drawn in the Cash Book. *Nearly all that he displays, with the exception of his moccasins and fur armband, is of white manufacture but has been selected and modified to reflect his Nez Perce affiliation. Photo courtesy of the Department of the Interior, National Park Service, Nez Perce National Historic Park, NEPE-HI-1171*

Left: Nez Perce warrior, detail from figure 24

My first personal contact with Native people occurred in 1967. As a skinny teenager in Boy Scout Troop 22, I accompanied my unit on a field trip to Spokane's Franklin Park for the annual Smoqueshin Days celebration sponsored by the Spokane Tribe. A front row seat on the lawn looked like a convenient place to watch the Snake Dance, which is what they called the Grand Entry in those days. An older Indian lady sitting in a lawn chair next to me opened the conversation. We talked about the weather, the Boy Scout group, my schooling, and as the dancers paraded by she pointed out certain individuals, relatives of hers, commenting on their outfits and their dancing. I responded politely but no doubt ignorantly. Despite my lack of knowledge about Native ways, or maybe because of it, we made appointments to meet on a somewhat regular basis to further our friendship by sharing information about ourselves as well as to provide lessons for me on traditional arts and culture of the Spokane Indian people.

Through my friendship with this lady, my education and circle of Native friends grew. Acquaintances from neighboring tribes spoke of concerns about their younger generation. The young people, it was said, were taken in by the allure of prize money at the contest dances held during powwows. They were being *Indians* certainly, but were emulating dancers and the clothing styles of other tribes to catch the attention of dance judges instead of carrying on the traditions of their grandparents. I, on the other hand, was interested in the old ways, the regional traditions, and was graciously given tutelage in what it was to be *Spokane, Umitilla,* and *Nez Perce.* These Native teachers encouraged me to write down what I was learning in the hope that the wayward youth would someday want to know what it meant to be Spokane or Nez Perce. You and your writing, I was charged, will help teach them. The accumulated facts, lore, resource people, and craft lessons from over twenty years spent in this avocational study provided me with a broad base of information. It was 1990 when Fortune gave me an opportunity to fulfill my charge. The work of a Nez Perce artist came my way via an Indian agent, his heirs, and a northern Idaho farming family now headed by Don Beck. Knowing of my interest in Northwest history and ethnology, Don asked if I would like to view some "Indian drawings" his mother possessed. Of course my answer was yes. The drawings contained unique and moving Native glimpses of events during a tragic war.

Thanks to the encouragement and education provided me by the elders, and the youngers, of the Northwest tribes, I've gained some valuable insight into the content of the drawing and am beginning to understand their emotional impact as well. I am honored to have the opportunity to present these drawings and their interpretations to a wider audience than would ever have been possible if circumstances had been such that the *Cash Book* had remained stored away instead of being reproduced in this book.

Acknowledgments

The opportunity to research and report on an item as interesting and historically important as the *Cash Book* and its content is rare indeed. This report could not have been completed without the help of a number of institutions and individuals who kindly fulfilled my requests for additional resources, information, and opinions. For assistance in establishing direction for my research and for help in obtaining background material, I wish to thank Robert Clark of the Arthur H. Clark Company, Spokane, Washington; Nancy Compo and the staff of the Northwest Room, Spokane Public Library, Spokane, Washington; Richard Fusick, National Archives, Washington, D.C., and Joyce Justice, also of the National Archives, Pacific Alaska Region, Seattle, Washington; the staff of the Glenbow Museum Archives, Calgary, Alberta; the Idaho State Historical Society staff; personnel of the Nez Perce National Historic Park, Spalding, Idaho, in particular Kevin Peters and Robert Applegate; Patricia McCormack, Provincial Museum of Alberta, Edmonton, Alberta; Art Randall of the Museum of North Idaho, Coeur d'Alene, Idaho; and the staff of the reference and interlibrary loan departments, Spokane County Library system, whose patience and diligence in fulfilling my numerous requests for obscure publications were commendable. In addition to all of the above, I am indebted to Lynn Bain and Janey Kuh for their proofreading and honest evaluations of my communication skills.

Help in interpreting the content of the drawings involved the largest number of people on my thank-you list. Those representing institutions include Sue Emory and George Hatley of the Appaloosa Museum and Heritage Center Foundation, Moscow, Idaho; Donald H. McTernan, Springfield Armory National Historic Site, Springfield, Massachusetts; Tim O'Gorman, U.S. Quartermaster Museum, Fort

Lee, Virginia; Lynn Pankonin, Cheney Cowles Museum, Spokane, Washington; and Doug Wicklund of the National Firearms Museum, Washington, D.C. All of these people represented their institutions honorably through their responses to my questions and their assessment of photographs of the *Cash Book* drawings which were provided them. The accommodations made to me by John Guido and his staff at the Holland Library Archives, Washington State University, Pullman, resulted in invaluable information gained through this institution's collection of the Lucullus V. McWhorter papers.

Among the individuals who contributed to this body of information, I will first recognize John Ewers, Deward E. Walker, Jr., and Alvin Josephy for their kind responses to my inquiries regarding the artistic and historic significance of the *Cash Book* drawings. My thanks for input and encouragement also go to Roger Ernesti, formerly of Wapato, Washington, whose long association with the Yakamas and Lakotas has given him a wealth of knowledge about these people; Richard Kuh, without whom valuable contemporary impressions of the Sun Dance scenes in the *Cash Book* could not have been obtained; George Kush, for his input on Nez Perce experiences in Canada; Terry Leaf, a student of military history who seems to have limitless resources on this topic; and Steven D. Shawley, whose untimely death prevented him from seeing the results of his contributions to my research regarding Nez Perce ethnology and material culture. All gave their time and expertise to enhance the interpretations of the drawings.

Input from the Indian people themselves was invaluable. Among the many who viewed and commented on the *Cash Book* drawings, I wish especially to recognize Horace Axtell, Nancy Halfmoon, and Dorothy Jackson, of the Nez Perce Nation; Calvin Jumping Bull and Severt Young Bear, Sr., both Lakota; and Lela Stevenson, of Lakota/Nez Perce heritage. I hope this publication will return their kind services by making the drawings and text available to them and to future generations of Indian people.

I greatly appreciate the encouragement and patience shown to me by Naomi Pascal, Julidta Tarver, and others on the staff of the University of Washington Press as they guided me through the process of publishing. Each question I asked of them was promptly and thoroughly answered, and each task I needed to complete was clearly and courteously explained. Bill Holm and Allen Pinkham, who reviewed the first draft of this book while it was still in the proposal stage, alerted me to several sections of the manuscript needing revision or emphasis. The comments and compliments of these two authorities on history and Native culture were welcome. I admire and appreciate editor Leila Charbonneau's attention to detail. Her suggestions and corrections were very helpful.

Finally my sincere thanks go to Mary Beck and her family for their concern for the preservation of the *Cash Book*, and their confidence in my ability to present its history and content so that others can learn from, and enjoy, the drawings it contains.

I Will Tell of

My War Story

A Pictorial Account

of the Nez Perce War

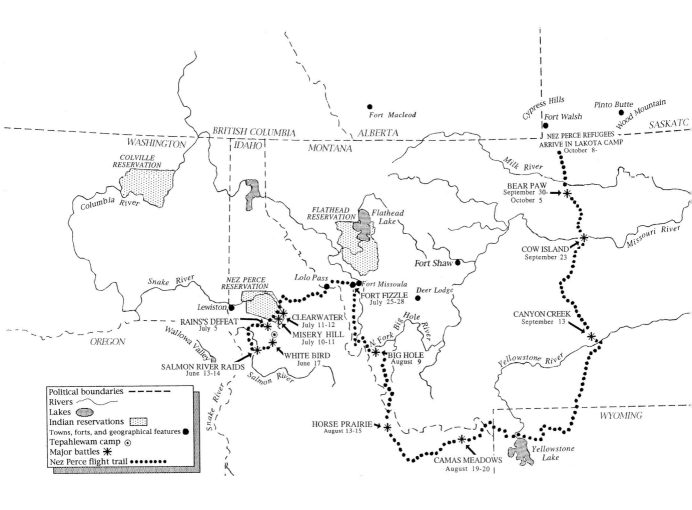

Events in the War Against the Nez Perce, 1877

Charles Warner's Cash Book

Its History and Preservation

Charles D. Warner served as the United States government's agent to the Nez Perce Indians of Idaho from March 1879 through June 1881.[1] Found among the papers Warner assembled during his tenure was a pocket notebook containing drawings, firsthand accounts of events during and after the 1877 Nez Perce war. These drawings are unique because they were produced by a Nez Perce warrior, a participant in the conflict, and show the Indian side of this bit of Northwest history. Fortunately for historians, ethnologists, interested individuals, and the descendants of those involved in the 1877 conflict, the little notebook was safeguarded and passed along by Warner. When he died, friends of the Warner family acquired and cared for the book, finally presenting it to the Idaho State Historical Society for preservation. Understanding the events surrounding the preservation and discovery of the *Cash Book*, as this little notebook was entitled, helps in interpreting its intent and content nearly as much as viewing the drawings themselves.

Sherman Avenue, the main street of downtown Coeur d'Alene, Idaho, runs roughly east and west. On Sherman, between Sixth and Seventh Streets, stood the house of Charles D. Warner and his wife, Anna. Across the street from the Warners lived Elizabeth and Robert Mann, who in time developed a close friendship with the Warners. This friendship eventually resulted in Mrs. Mann's acquisition of Charles Warner's estate, including his collection of papers, memorabilia, and the *Cash Book* with its historic drawings.[2]

The information available on Warner's life and his role in Idaho history is sketchy. He was born in Cambridge, New York, July 18, 1840, to Solomon and Eliza Warner. He finished his schooling at Eastman business college, also in New York, and began a

3

Charles D. Warner

Anna Warner

career in a foundry and machine shop, the same occupation in which his father was engaged. At the outbreak of the Civil War, young men, including Warner, were called from their chosen careers, or felt compelled to volunteer, to fill the ranks of the Union army. Holding the position of quartermaster sergeant in the 123rd New York Infantry, Warner saw action at Gettysburg and served under Sherman in other engagements. During his tour of duty, he married Anna Green in 1864. His service apparently ended without promotion, for he still held the rank of sergeant.

Warner's activities and adventures after his discharge from the military have not yet come to light. The designation "Major" with which in later life he often prefixed his signature did not reflect his Civil War status but was a title of respect, and especially authority, acquired as a result of his appointment in 1879 to the office of Indian Agent, Nez Perce Agency, Lapwai, Idaho. Clark Wissler explained the phenomenon this way: "On the reservation, the most

talked-about person was 'The Major'. The Indian Bureau addressed him as Agent, but locally, he was Major. This had at least one virtue, for though agents came and went with surprising frequency, the Major went on forever. So far as my observations go most of the incumbents of that office liked the title."[3]

Though Warner's appointment missed the dangers and intrigue of the Nez Perce war itself, he inherited the aftereffects from the former agent, John B. Monteith. Warner's tenure lasted through June 1882, when he was "relieved of duty as Agent."[4] The reason for his departure was no doubt political, but whatever the cause another Monteith was named to succeed him. This time it was Charles Monteith, the former agent's brother. Charles Monteith had prior agency experience as superintendent of farming and agency clerk under his brother, with "secretarial affairs" as his main concern.[5] After his departure from the Nez Perce Agency, Warner received an endorsement from John B. Neil, then governor of Idaho territory, to continue service in the Indian Department. It seems an agency position in Alaska was in the offing, but preferring to remain in the Pacific Northwest, Warner declined this offer in favor of developing mining claims along the Columbia River.[6]

Eventually, Warner acquired employment in Coeur d'Alene, Idaho, where he served as weather observer, keeping records for government files. He spent several years as receiver in the United States Land Office, and operated a general store as well. His store mainly served the men and families stationed at Fort Sherman (known as Fort Coeur d'Alene prior to 1891), which was established as a military post in 1879.[7] Warner is noted as one of the original incorporators of Coeur d'Alene. During those years, Mrs. Warner worked as postmistress for Spirit Lake, Idaho, which included all of the Coeur d'Alene addresses, and was instrumental in founding the First Presbyterian Church of Coeur d'Alene.[8]

After retirement from these responsibilities, the aging Warners kept their residence in Coeur d'Alene. Elizabeth Mann, their neighbor, cared for the elderly couple, bringing them baked goods and running errands to the post office and grocery store. Mrs. Mann kindly listened to Warner's reminiscences, and especially enjoyed those recounting his experiences as agent among the Nez Perce Indians. In the months after Anna Warner's death, Mrs. Mann continued to care for Charles Warner until he also died. Warner's obituary in the *Coeur d'Alene Press*, dated Saturday, March 27, 1920, reads:

> After surviving his wife nine weeks, Major C. D. Warner, this morning at 6:45, passed away, the cause of death being saline debility.
>
> Major Warner left no known relatives, but a host of friends.
>
> He was born July 18, 1840, and married Anna A. Green, March 1, 1864. He was quartermaster sergeant

in the 123rd New York Volunteers of the Army of the Potomac.

> He came to Coeur d'Alene in 1887 and was post trade in this city, and later receiver of the land office for nine years and has kept the weather report without compensation from the government for a number of years. He took an active part in the affairs of the city, county and state. Major Warner was past commander of Temple Commandery No. 8 and the funeral services which will be conducted tomorrow from the Masonic temple, will be the ritualistic Commandery services. The body will be taken from the Mooney parlors to the Temple at 1 o'clock.

As a result of Elizabeth Mann's kindness, and since no immediate heirs existed, Major Warner bequeathed his estate and his collection of papers to her family. Included with Warner's papers were narratives he had recorded from Nez Perce storytellers and headmen, and the small leather-covered booklet entitled *Cash Book*, containing drawings of the Nez Perce war. The booklet received its name from the India ink inscription on its cover, which states simply "Cash Book."

Charles Warner's papers, including the *Cash Book*, were stored in a trunk which eventually passed from Elizabeth Mann to her daughter, Margaret Ott. The trunk itself was sold, being considered excess clutter, but fortunately Mrs. Ott kept Warner's papers and memorabilia. These were placed in a manila envelope and kept in a kitchen drawer. Every so often, the "Indian drawings," as the family called them, would be brought out as a novelty to "show off to the kids," but for the most part they were kept in the drawer.

Later in life, Mrs. Ott was diagnosed as having Alzheimer's disease. Her niece, Mary Beck (Elizabeth Mann's granddaughter), helped move Mrs. Ott to a place where she could receive the necessary care.

Mary Beck

The packet of Warner memorabilia, the legends, letters, and the Indian drawings, came into the possession of the Beck family as a result of this move.[9]

I enter the story rather late in its history. On December 24, 1990, Don Beck, Mary Beck's son, got in touch with me about some snapshots the family had taken of the Indian-drawn images from the *Cash Book*. He wished to know more about the drawings and, aware of my interest in local Native history and culture, thought I was the person to contact. Don supposed the drawings were of Nez Perce origin and knew they had been collected by a family friend named Major Warner, who he had been told at one time worked as an agent at the Nez Perce reservation.

Leafing through the snapshots was much like opening a stack of presents, for each photo offered a new surprise. First to catch my attention were the drawings of Indians in combat with blue-uniformed soldiers. Phonetically spelled names of several principal characters from the Nez Perce war of 1877 accompanied some of the drawings. Also recognizable was a Lakota Sun Dance camp. Putting these three bits of information together left little doubt that these drawings were produced by an individual recording events related to the Nez Perce war. Views of a Lakota Sun Dance and explicit hand-to-hand combat scenes of Nez Perce warriors and soldiers convinced me that the artist had firsthand knowledge of these events and was probably one of the participants who survived the battles and managed to escape to Sitting Bull's Lakota camp in Canada. He would have had to stay in Canada with the Lakota as a refugee for at least a year in order to witness a Sun Dance during the summer months, and he eventually must have made his way back to the Nez Perce reservation in Lapwai, Idaho, in order for this pocket notebook and drawings to find their way into Warner's possession.

Initial research was conducted through the early months of 1991 to identify more of the names written in the *Cash Book*. Each new discovery during the detective work added to the excitement and energy generated by the project. Copies of my findings were given to Don to deliver to his mother, who still had possession of the little booklet. Both Don and his mother now realized the historical importance of the pictographic drawings and of Warner's other documents and asked that I help determine the best place for the family to donate the Warner collection.

The contents of the *Cash Book* were shared with Lynn Pankonin of the Eastern Washington State Historical Society in Spokane, and Steve Shawley, formerly of the National Park Service, who resided in Lewiston, Idaho. Both Steve and Lynn, though eager to keep the little book as close at hand as possible, admitted that the best place to house it and the accompanying papers would probably be with the Idaho State Historical Society, located in Boise. There, the *Cash Book*, as well as the rest of the Warner papers, would be documented and available to serious researchers but preserved from general wear and the deteriorating effects of light and moisture.

As part of the Historical Society collection there would be no chance of the items disappearing from public access into a private collection. "In addition," explained Steve Shawley, "most researchers and others think of Idaho when they think of the Nez Perce." For these reasons, Idaho was suggested as the most logical state to receive the Warner materials. Mrs. Beck accepted the recommendation, and the *Cash Book* has since been turned over to the Idaho State Historical Society.[10]

Prior to the decision to donate the Warner papers to the Historical Society, arrangements were made to have Mrs. Beck relate the history of the Warner papers and give her interpretation of their content. During these interviews (several sessions were necessary to complete the job), I photocopied Warner's handwritten narratives and inspected and photographed each page of the *Cash Book*.

The *Cash Book* is a commercially made pocket notebook with calfskin covers. Closed, the book measures $2^{3/4}$ by $4^{5/8}$ inches (about 7 by 12 centimeters). It contains twenty-eight leaves held together by a sewn binding. The leaves are of medium quality paper and have no watermark or other identification evident. Effects of age are showing in some discoloration and brittleness of the paper. One leaf (figures 9 and 10) has separated from the binding but is still in its proper sequence. All leaves are ruled with sixteen blue horizontal lines. One red vertical line marks the left margin of each leaf and two red lines form a column at the right margin. Some notations in India ink appearing on at least sixteen pages throughout the book refer to men, women, and horses. Most of these notes, unlike other writing in the book, seem to have no relation to the drawings. The words "Cash Book" written on the front cover, and the India ink notations, suggest that the book may originally have been purchased and prepared for

an accounting job related to Nez Perce agency business. I can imagine an agency employee preparing the headings for his accounting job, but then deciding to take advantage of an opportunity to have one of the participants of the recent war recount his experiences in pictures, so the book was handed over to an Indian artist to chronicle his involvement in the 1877 conflict. This little scenario is speculation until more information comes to light regarding the history of the *Cash Book*.

Mary Beck gives Major Warner the credit not only for preserving the drawings but for soliciting them as well. Warner did record several Nez Perce speeches and legends and pass his collected materials on to Elizabeth Mann. The drawings, however, may have been made under the supervision or direction of another agency employee, possibly clerk G. D. Fleming, who eventually gave the book to Warner. Fleming's title was Superintendent of Farming, a job he held from late 1881 through June 1892.[11] Certainly this job, like the one held by Charles Monteith, involved some clerical responsibilities. A cash book was an item more likely to be used by a clerk than an administrator. The style of writing within the book supports this assumption. Comparing Major Warner's script as it appears on his other papers and on an insert within the *Cash Book* with the writing on the pages of the *Cash Book* leaves no doubt that Warner was not the person who wrote the headings or the other words in the book. Further, according to Lucullus McWhorter (1860–1944), author and historian of the Nez Perce war, Fleming was instrumental in securing safe homes for fugitive Nez Perce returning from Canada after the war:

During my incumbency [Fleming told McWhorter], many of the Nez Perce war band who escaped from General Miles at the last battle and made their homes with the Sioux, Blackfeet, and other tribes, drifted back to the Nez Perce Reservation. These "hostiles," as so termed, were all known to the Indian Police, who arrested and brought them into the agency as soon as discovered. Coming before me, I was supposed to turn them over to the Agent, whose duty was to deliver them to the military post commander, to be transported to the Indian Territory. I have always been glad that in no instance did I ever do this. I would talk to the prisoner, who never failed to show anxiety to be accorded a chance to prove a sincerity of intentions to be law-abiding and peaceable. I would then turn to the Indian police, pointing to the fact that the refugee had suffered enough; that there was nothing to be gained by holding him (or her) prisoner, to be sent so far from their old home and people; that they were full willing to abide by the laws of the Reservation as prescribed by the Government; and I requested that the brother or sister be turned loose, which was invariably done.

Not once did any of these forlorn outcasts prove recreant to the trust placed in their promises. They had fought and lost! Returning broken in spirit and in purse, they stoically accepted the inevitable, burying the dead past.[12]

Fleming also noted that Warner had little to do with judging conflicts that arose between reservation Indians. Fleming's job, as this evidence indicates, involved working closely with the Nez Perce people, including the returning refugees. His compassion for their situation would place him in an excellent position to receive information on the war itself. Warner, however, was the head administrator, and though he definitely deserves the credit for establishing a climate of benevolence, the facts at hand do not point to him as the individual in direct contact with the *Cash Book* artist.

Government policy in Warner's day was directed toward assimilating Indians into white culture by teaching them agriculture, insisting on a Christian view of the world, and doing away with traditional tribal practices and dress. Outwardly, he had to comply with Indian Office policy. Any benevolent feelings he had toward his Nez Perce depended on the behavior of his wards. Warner officially praised his "civilized" reservation Nez Perce, as he called them, for chasing off "those wearing blankets and holding to Indian customs" from an Independence Day celebration. As the "civilized" Christian Nez Perce expressed it, "No *Indians* were allowed" at this celebration. Warner, his duty being to enforce government policy, used the terms "civilized" or "friendly" Indians, as compared to the "hostiles," to identify tribal factions in a report referring to government reimbursement for acquisition of horses used in the 1877 war effort.[13]

In addition to those Nez Perce already on the Lapwai reservation, Chief Joseph's captured Nez Perce being detained in Indian Territory (now Oklahoma) were petitioning for return to their homeland at Lapwai. Officially, Warner claimed that he did not want Joseph's people returned to the Lapwai reserve. It was feared that trouble would result if the hostile, nontreaty Nez Perce were brought back to Idaho. Whites in the country surrounding Lapwai were talking of taking punitive action against any Nez Perce brought back to the reservation.[14]

This story, however, is not so much about those Nez Perce who were interned in Indian Territory but about those who fought and died, and those who escaped the final battlefield and fled to asylum in Canada. As months and years went by, homesick refugees drifted back to Idaho from Canada. Some were permitted to stay on the reservation only so long as they renounced their traditional ways and followed the Indian Bureau's steps toward acculturation. Mary Beck feels, as I do, that Warner may have been outwardly complying with his supervisor's policy toward Indians of insisting on acculturation and issuing punishment for resisting, in order to keep his position as agent, regardless of what he felt was morally correct.

But Warner did not maintain a completely insensitive front. He seemed to have good rapport with the leaders and elders on the reservation.[15] In a communiqué to his superior, E. A. Hayt, Commissioner of Indian Affairs, Warner presented a petition from reservation headmen requesting that "members of 'Joseph's' band who have been with the 'Sioux' since the Surrender of Joseph be allowed to return to this reservation and their homes."[16] Concerns of these headmen were expressed in a speech by an elder, Shu Yai, which Warner recorded on the spot, hurriedly writing as interpreter Perrin Whitman translated from Nez Perce to English.

> Yes, my Agent, as you are *going* to leave here and go to Washington where all the head men are gathered together. As you are talking your heart over there, as yours and mine. Long time ago one man had charge of all the people now as you Agent today all just the same as him, and know all the hearts of each man. And as God has joined us together and he possess the earth with people, and you, Agent, to day are, and like it trying to civilize the people in all manner of work, and now is no talk about that. We will join hands before we separated, therefore I show my heart to the head men where you are *going* and leaving each other as we old men. We part as for one day. You are *going* and I stay hear, and I do not wish to hear of any whites over me until you come back. Then we will meet and talk it all over, and as you are agent to Joseph country, we would like to have you bring all the children back with you whose parents are here.[17]

Shu Yai had several concerns he wished his agent, Warner, to faithfully convey to the headmen in Washington, D.C. Shu Yai wondered about unfulfilled treaty promises regarding the civilizing of his people. He worried that Warner might leave his post and be replaced by a less understanding agent. Maybe Shu Yai was recalling the temperament of the former agent, John B. Monteith. If Warner was replaced, as often happened with agents, the new appointee might be as rigid in his ethnocentric convictions as Charles Monteith, who had favored Christianized Nez Perce and disdained traditionalists, thus helping to set the stage for the 1877 war. Finally, Shu Yai was thinking of the self-exiled Nez Perce, those who made good their escape to Canada from the siege at the foot of the Bear Paw Mountains of Montana. He wanted assurance of their safe return home to Lapwai to rejoin their families.

Although most of the warring Nez Perce were sent to Indian Territory, or *Ekish Pah*—the Hot Place, as the captive Nez Perce called it—those who managed to escape and secure refuge with Sitting Bull's Sioux, or *Lakota*, in Canada were obviously on Shu Yai's and Warner's minds. And some of those refugees did return to Lapwai even without the government's approval. One was an artist. Chronicled in pictorial form on the pages of a little ledger with the words "Cash Book" written on its cover is the story of this artist and his people.

Notes

1. Erwin N. Thompson, *Historic Resource Study: Spalding Area* (Denver: National Park Service, U.S. Department of the Interior, 1972), 160; Clifford M. Drury, *Henry Harmon Spalding* (Caldwell: Caxton, 1936), 427.

2. Mary Beck, personal interview, 6 June and 15 December 1992.

3. James H. Hawley, *History of Idaho: The Gem of the Mountains* (Chicago: S. J. Clarke, 1920), 243; Clark Wissler, *Indian Cavalcade, or Life on the Old-time Indian Reservations* (New York: Sheridan House, 1938), 24.

4. *Biographical and Historical Index of American Indians and Persons Involved in Indian Affairs* (Boston: G. K. Hall, 1966), 337; Frances Whitman Monteith, "Indian Troubles and Treaties," manuscript, Spokane Public Library, North West Room, n.d.

5. Thompson, *Historic Resource Study*, 160.

6. Beck, interview, 6 June 1992; Mary Beck to author, 1 February 1993; Hawley, *History of Idaho*, 293.

7. Hawley, *History of Idaho*, 558–61.

8. Art Randall to author, Museum of North Idaho, 13 January 1993.

9. M. Beck to author, 1 February 1993.

10. Steven D. Shawley, personal interview, 10 November 1991; Idaho State Historical Society Library and Archives, Charles D. Warner collection, MS 2-1053.

11. Joyce Justice (National Archives: Pacific Northwest Region) to author, 22 February 1993; "Payroll Accounts, 1881, Nez Perce Agency, Lapwai, ID," National Archives, Pacific Alaska Region (Seattle). Though circumstances point to Fleming's involvement in the production of the *Cash Book* drawings, other possibilities must be considered: the *Cash Book* may have been produced en route during the 1877 war and had no reservation connections; the drawings may have been produced well after the war and could have been obtained by Warner during any of his post-agent activities. Statements obtained from the Beck family and Warner's agency-era papers found accompanying the *Cash Book* support the view that the drawings were produced on the Nez Perce reservation during Warner's tenure as Indian agent.

12. From a personal interview of Fleming conducted by McWhorter and quoted in Lucullus McWhorter, *Yellow Wolf: His Own Story* (Caldwell: Caxton, 1983), 291.

13. Charles D. Warner, "Lapwai Agency," *Annual Report of the Commissioner of Indian Affairs*, Executive Document I (Washington, D.C.: Government Printing Office, 1879), 163.

14. Thompson, *Historic Resource Study*, 159.

15. Writer Alvin Josephy credits Warner for this innovative process of gathering councils of all adult Nez Perce males, not just headmen, for the purpose of gaining a broad-based understanding of tribal needs and concerns. Alvin M. Josephy, *Chief Joseph's People and Their War* (Yellowstone National Park: The Yellowstone Association, 1964), 160. Warner's rapport with the Nez Perce is further shown by a commentary he was able to obtain from Eagle of the Light, who during the war was noted for his near-hostile attitude toward settled reservation life. Eagle of the Light, "Speech of Eagle of the Light," manuscript, M. Beck Collection; Jack Holterman, *The Eagle from the Rising Sun* (West Glacier: Glacier Natural History Association, 1991); David Lavender, *Let Me Be Free* (New York: HarperCollins, 1992), 165, 166, 201; Lucullus McWhorter, *Hear Me, My Chiefs!* (1952; Caldwell: Caxton, 1986), 108.

16. Charles D. Warner to E. A. Hayt, Commissioner of Indian Affairs, May 26, 1879, "Petition for return of Joseph's followers Now among the Sioux," National Archives, Collection RG 75, Microfilm Copy M 234, Roll 351, Records of the Bureau of Indian Affairs, 1879, P 104-w2625, pp. 0569–0572.

17. "Speech of Shu-yai, (Unpainted)," manuscript, M. Beck Collection, 1881. The word *manuscript* is almost too kind to describe Warner's scrawl. It is no easy task to read Warner's writing under normal conditions, but this and the two other speeches made by Nez Perce headmen and recorded by Warner seem to have been written more hurriedly than other papers in Warner's collection. Shu Yai's quote varies from the original in two ways. Warner's manuscript lacks any punctuation. The inclusion of punctuation was based on the consensus of a group of educators and historians who reviewed all of the Warner manuscripts. These reviewers included Rick Kuh, Colville, Washington; Lynn Bain, Writing Specialist, Spokane Public Schools, Spokane, Washington; Dr. Mark Lester, Eastern Washington State University, Cheney; and the writer. Several words in Warner's manuscript are indecipherable. Judging from the relative length of these words and the context, decisions were made by the same group to enter "best guess" words, which are printed in italic.

Nontreaty Life

An Overview of

Traditional Nez Perce Culture

Before departing on a study of the *Cash Book* and its individual drawings, an overview of Nez Perce culture and of the 1877 war is necessary to understand and appreciate the pictorial messages the *Cash Book* artist was trying to convey. Few literary sources are readily available which pertain to the culture of the Nez Perce people. As of this writing the works of Deward E. Walker, especially *Indians of Idaho* (1978), are probably the most accessible and reliable, based in part on fieldwork with the Nez Perce people. Carolyn James's *Nez Perce Women in Transition, 1877–1990* (1996) focuses on women and their views of Native culture and is drawn almost entirely from the comments of interviewees. Interesting accounts of Nez Perce culture and history as well as characteristic photographs are contained in Edward Curtis's *The North American Indian* (1911). *The Nez Perce Indians* (1908), Herbert Spinden's ethnological report, is rather technical in nature and open to mild criticism regarding accuracy. Although limited mainly to material culture, Steven D. Shawley's "Nez Perce Dress" (1974) is based on extensive association with Nez Perce arts and artifacts, and the people themselves. These last three works are not readily available from most lending libraries. On the other hand, a collection of books about Nez Perce history, in particular the 1877 war, could occupy a disproportionate amount of shelf space in one's library. Considering ease in reading, accessibility, and reliable content, Mark H. Brown's *The Flight of the Nez Perce* (1967) and Alvin Josephy's *The Nez Perce Indians and the Opening of the Northwest* (1965) rate highly. Two of Lucullus McWhorter's works, *Hear Me, My Chiefs!* (1952) and *Yellow Wolf: His Own Story* (1940), though compiled from informants nearly fifty years after the conflict, are well researched and provide valuable insight from the Indian point of view. These books, collectively, do an adequate job of presenting the background and history of the Nez Perce war, as well as providing information about Nez Perce culture. Most others, well written or not, offer no new information or interpretations of these topics. A brief review of the information contained in the above-listed sources, a few others included, should sufficiently set the stage for a better understanding of the *Cash Book* drawings.

The Nez Perce live in a region labeled the Plateau culture area by students and anthropologists. This area is bounded by the Cascade Mountains on the west and the Rocky Mountains on the east. Within these longitudinal bounds the Plateau encompasses the majority of the Fraser River and Columbia River drainage. Most anthropological works published in the early 1900s and before dismissed the Plateau region as a simple mixture of Northwest Coast and Plains cultural traits. More recent researchers specializing in the Plateau geographic area were able to discern unique characteristics.[1]

Subsistence patterns, for the most part, followed an annual cycle of activities emphasizing gathering roots and berries and fishing for salmon. A few bands added variety to their diets and adventure to their lives by mounting expeditions over the Rocky Mountains to the Plains in quest of bison.

Social and political life centered on the smaller population units of villages and bands. The concept of a single tribal chief was not part of the Plateau system. Leadership remained local and specialized, shifting from one individual to another depending on the activity needing direction and on the skills of the available leaders. Material culture and decorative art styles were fairly consistent throughout the Plateau. It is no surprise that the *Cash Book* artist identifies his subjects through these regional styles and conventions. Religious beliefs characteristic of the Plateau, especially the guardian spirit concept

and the ʔipnuʼ cililpt faith, influenced several of the *Cash Book* artist's choice of topics.

The world of the Plateau people and of the Nez Perce in particular was not a world limited to a person's physical senses. Power or spirits abounded in all things: rocks, wind, insects, water, and all animals. These spirits might, if they chose, select a human to befriend and with whom they would share their special powers. Unlike the Plains people who initiated a quest for a spirit helper, the Plateau people had to be patient, sometimes waiting years until a spirit made the decision to contact them. "There were times when our families walked us through steps to become chosen," notes Francis Cullooya, "Not a quest. We were chosen. An animal spirit helper chose us. It gave us a song to help us in time of need."[2]

Contact between the spirit and the human might happen at any time, but most often it was the human who prepared the way for the initial contact. Around puberty, a youth would be spiritually prepared by a holy or medicine person and sent to a place that spirits were known to frequent. If the youth was lucky, he or she might be contacted by a powerful spirit, and with this contact would be given certain powers possessed or controlled by the spirit. Such powers as healing the sick, changing the weather, finding game, and avoiding injury in battle were considered useful and desirable.[3] One of the more powerful and hoped-for spirit helpers for warriors was the wolf. Noted for his quickness, cunning, and ferocity—all desirable qualities for a warrior—wolf also was a member of a hunting team, the pack. The Nez Perce method of warfare was similar to the way wolf hunted with his pack. Though every warrior was free to make his own choices about methods of attack, it was their combined efforts that brought the tribe favorable results in many a tough situation. Emblems of wolf power are pictured throughout the *Cash Book*, usually in the form of a wolf hide suspended from a coat or cloak.

Individuals may have additional spirit helpers which impart powers less general and more personal than wolf's warrior medicine. Along with any gift of power came certain conditions, a frequent one being a restriction on overtly advertising the natural spirit that gave the power. Even so, the *Cash Book* artist included a drawing of what seems to be a warrior's spirit helper, probably in order to aid the viewer in correctly identifying the individual (see figure 12).

A second aspect of Plateau religion, but one clearly separate from aid imparted by a spirit helper, had common roots with a religious movement spurred on by the teachings of a Wanapum named Smohalla. A version of this religion was promoted among the Nez Perce and Palouse people by noted visionaries such as Somilppilp, Husus Kute, and Toohoolhoolzote.[4] Adherents believed that on a certain calling, determined by the Creator, they would die and remain dead, in an unconscious-like state, for three to five days. During this time, their spirit would visit the land of the Creator to receive teachings and doctrine which needed to be communicated to those still living. When these teachings had been learned, the spirit of the dead or unconscious person would return to the body, the body would come back to life, and thus be able to deliver those messages. This idea of the spirit leaving the body to receive messages from the Creator is believed to be an ancient one revived, some say, due to pressures of white expansion. The whites called this religion the Dreamer religion, but to the Nez Perce it was the Washani or ʔipnu' cililpt faith.[5]

Among other things, ʔipnu' cililpt teachings included a special regard for the earth. (These teachings are still alive and developing, known today as the Seven Drum religion.[6]) ʔipnu' cililpt beliefs would not accommodate the idea of individual ownership of parcels of land. Nor could the followers of this faith accept the agrarian concept of plowing and planting, of forcing the land to grow crops not native to the region. The Nez Perce's reverence for the sacredness of the earth caused obvious difficulties during treaty negotiations with whites who viewed land as something individuals could possess and manipulate. As if matters between the Nez Perce ʔipnu' cililpt followers and whites were not complicated enough, a third group of people compounded the problems of landownership. These were the Christian Nez Perce. Protestant missionaries working with the Nez Perce, notably Henry Harmon Spalding and Asa Smith, encouraged an agrarian lifestyle. Along with Christian doctrine, permanent residences and other aspects of white culture were emphasized as the way toward acculturation and salvation. Nez Perce Indian Agent John B. Monteith continued practicing these philosophies with his own religious zeal, recognizing the worth of his Christianized Nez Perce while trying to bring the so-called heathen traditionalists under his control. The civilized or Christian Nez Perce were the ones the ʔipnu' cililpt believers blamed for originally and continually giving up the land during treaty negotiations. It was the Christianized Indians and their prewar government agents who showed no tolerance or sympathy to the Dreamers, going so far as to try demanding conversion to Christianity before being allowed to settle on the reservation.[7]

Further misunderstandings and trouble came because of the ʔipnu' cililpt belief that if the truly faithful followers kept performing the communal ritual and dance which was the outward profession of their faith, the world would renew itself to resemble earlier times. Bison and other game would again roam in uncountable herds, loved ones who had passed away would return to enjoy the fruits of this renewed earth, and the whites—the antagonists who caused the unwelcome changes in the Indians' world—would vanish from the land. As if to assert his association with the ?ipnu' cililpt faith, the *Cash Book* artist devotes three drawings early in his sketch book to scenes related to his beliefs.

Differences in Nez Perce religious beliefs were emphasized outwardly. Christian Indians had their hair cut short and wore clothes in the style of the white folks living around them. The followers of the ?ipnu' cililpt, on the other hand, wore what is now called *traditional* clothing. Dresses, leggings, shirts, and ornaments made from mostly white-manufactured goods but cut and tailored in an aboriginal way defined the clothing style of the ?ipnu' cililpt followers. The *Cash Book* artist clearly shows how white trade goods were adapted into the traditional Nez Perce culture. But the traditional way did not necessarily limit cultural traits to the common Plateau style. The Nez Perce borrowed ideas for clothing as well as political organization from tribes living on the Great Plains. This outward appearance was one of the reasons earlier anthropologists assumed that the culture of the Plateau tribes had no character of its own, but was a transitional area between the Northwest Coast and the Plains.

Verne Ray and Steven D. Shawley, however, revealed that Plains cultural traits which some Nez Perce bands exhibited—such as the glorification of war exploits and militaristic political organization—were only acquired traits masking truer Plateau traditions.[8]

One major way Plains cultural traits were acquired was through the practice some Nez Perce bands had of traveling to the Great Plains to hunt bison. Contact with the Plains tribes through cooperative hunts, trading sessions, and even warfare during these annual trips prompted an exchange of ideas and material culture. Ideas borrowed from Plains tribes can be seen in the decorative arts produced by the bison-hunting Nez Perce themselves. They began to look and act a bit more like their Plains associates. The *Cash Book* artist shows these Plains influences over and over again in depictions of warrior regalia—feather bonnets, shields, and honor marks emblazoned on the flanks of the warriors' horses. Evident also in this hunting-oriented faction of Nez Perce culture was a militaristic organization of the camp when on the move, especially when away from home territory in pursuit of bison.[9]

Plains groups such as the Lakota, Cheyenne, and Blackfeet more often than not looked upon the Nez Perce and their Plateau allies as intruders on their bison grounds and used this as an excuse, if any was needed, to raid or attack the allied Plateau camps and hunting parties. For the Plains tribes, successful war exploits were the way to wealth and upward social mobility. The Plains people's desire for war honors to enhance individual status, aspirations of quick wealth by raiding Plateau horse herds, and territorial jealousy regarding tribal hunting rights on certain bison grounds all gave the bison-hunting Nez Perce cause to establish strong defensive strategies.[10] A moving camp would be organized for defense[11]; scouts rode one to three miles in advance of the main band, followed by the headmen. The women, children, and elderly, along with horses laden with equipment, traveled in the center of the group, while strung out behind were additional horses being driven, usually, by youths not yet of warrior age. To the rear were warriors, with more scouts out to the flanks protecting the band's main store of wealth, the horse herd. Several chiefs—or more correctly, headmen—presided over the band while on the Plains and while moving to and from the bison-hunting grounds. These headmen, sometimes called war chiefs, were recognized as individuals experienced in warfare and defense of the camp. Acquisition of their leadership positions was based on these experiences but their tenure as leaders was often limited to times of danger, such as when the tribe was near enemies.

The rigorous demands of leadership while on bison hunts required a division of chiefly duties. While some used their talents as war chiefs, others put their skills to work as civil chiefs. Away from home territory, the civil chief helped organize the camp. He saw to the efficient setting up and taking down of tipis, packing of gear, and caring for the women, youngsters, and elderly.[12] It was this system developed by experience on the bison-hunting grounds that may well have given the Nez Perce the disciplined training and practice necessary in 1877 to hold off the U.S. troops as long as they did.[13]

Conflicts with other tribes were an accepted condition for life on the bison range. But war with the whites seemed slow to start considering the many injustices committed by whites against the Nez Perce. Some attribute Nez Perce inaction to pacifism, a societal trait said to be one which helps distinguish the Plateau from other culture areas.[14] Benjamin Bonneville wrote of his experiences with the Nez Perce, lamenting the inaction of a combined Nez Perce and Flathead bison-hunting party after their horse herd had been decimated three times by the Blackfeet.[15] True, the terms *war* and *conflict* didn't always fit nicely with the cooperative spirit needed for large intertribal salmon or root harvests, or for maintaining trade relations within the geographic area. But the term *pacifism* does not fit Plateau or Nez Perce attitudes either.[16] Oratory, restitutional gift giving, and, as legend has it, the gambling contest now called the stick game were accepted ways to

avoid intergroup, even intertribal, conflict and settle disputes.[17] But whether due to traditions of conflict avoidance, or more likely a combination of indecision and strategic choices in the face of a powerful foe, the "nontreaty" Nez Perce for a time postponed conflict with the whites.[18]

Notes

1. Verne F. Ray, *Cultural Relations in the Plateau of Northwestern America* (Los Angeles: The Southwest Museum, 1939), 1–3.

2. Francis Cullooya, "Spirituality and Sacred Ways," lecture delivered at Spokane Falls Community College, 26 September 1992.

3. Herbert J. Spinden, *The Nez Perce Indians* (Lancaster: New Era, 1908), 247–49; R. L. Packard, "Notes on the Mythology and Religion of Nez Perces," *Journal of American Folklore* 4 (1891): 328–30.

4. James Mooney, *The Ghost Dance Religion and the Sioux Outbreak of 1890*, Bureau of American Ethnology, 14th Annual Report, pt. 2 (Washington, D.C.: Government Printing Office, 1896), 711; Leslie Spier, *The Prophet Dance of the Northwest and Its Derivatives: The Source of the Ghost Dance* (Menasha: George Banta, 1935), 46.

5. Deward E. Walker, Jr., *Conflict and Schism in Nez Perce Acculturation* (Moscow: University of Idaho Press, 1985); Haruo Aoki, *Nez Perce Dictionary* (Berkeley: University of California Press, 1994), 33. Contemporary Nez Perce use the term *Walahsat* as well as "Seven Drum" when speaking of their religion; again see Aoki, 1266; Horace Axtell and Margo Aragon, *A Little Bit of Wisdom* (Lewiston: Confluence, 1997), 18.

6. Mari Watters, "Seven Drum Religion Remains Important to Plateau Indians," *Response*, June 1985, 14–15, 35.

7. McWhorter, *Yellow Wolf*, 290. See Walker, *Conflict and Schism*, for details on the complexities of these various factions. In reality, lines drawn by political and religious loyalties were not always distinct. Nearly every Nez Perce had relatives loyal to the opposing side. A few individuals, even some families, drifted on and off the reservation, spending time with both factions.

8. Ray, *Cultural Relations*, 1–3, 40, 145; Verne F. Ray, "Ethnohistory of the Joseph Band of Nez Perce Indians: 1805–1905," in *Nez Perce Indians* (New York: Garland, 1974), 173; Verne F. Ray, "Native Villages and Groupings of the Columbia Basin," *Pacific Northwest Quarterly* 27, no. 2 (1936): 99–152; Erna Gunther, "The Westward Movement of Some Plains Traits," *American Anthropologist* 52, no. 2 (1950): 174–80; Steven D. Shawley, "Nez Perce Dress: A Study in Cultural Change" (master's thesis, University of Idaho, 1974), 294.

9. For further information on how Plains cultural traits were incorporated into the Plateau system, see Ray, "Ethnohistory," 110, 111; Shawley, "Nez Perce Dress," 32, 49, 155, 258; Mark H. Brown, *The Flight of the Nez Perce* (Lincoln: University of Nebraska Press, 1967), 21; Bruce Hampton, *Children of Grace* (New York: Henry Holt, 1994), 21; Bruce A. Wilson, *From Where the Sun Now Stands* (Omak: Omak Chronicle, 1960), 11, 38.

10. Angelo Anastasio, "Southern Plateau: An Ecological Analysis of Intergroup Relations," *Northwest Anthropological Research Notes* 2 (Fall 1972): 109–228; Clifford M. Drury, *Chief Lawyer of the Nez Perce Indians* (Glendale: Arthur H. Clark, 1979), 76; Nicolas Point, S. J., *Wilderness Kingdom* (Chicago: Loyola University Press, 1967), 189; Washington Irving, *Adventures of Captain Bonneville, U.S.A., in the Rocky Mountains and the Far West* (Norman: University of Oklahoma Press, 1961), 106, 107.

11. John C. Ewers, *The Horse in Blackfoot Indian Culture* (Washington, D.C.: Smithsonian Institution Press, 1980), 143; Hampton, *Children of Grace*, 224.

12. Spinden, *Nez Perce Indians*, 226; Shawley, "Nez Perce Dress," 258; Lavender, *Let Me Be Free*, 252; Deward Walker, *Indians of Idaho* (Moscow: University of Idaho, 1978), 198.

13. Assessments of Nez Perce fighting ability based on their performance in the 1877 conflict can be found in Theodore Goldin, *A Bit of the Nez Perce Campaign* (Bryan: Theodore Goldin, 1978), 18; George O. Shields, *The Battle of the Big Hole* (Chicago: Rand McNally, 1889), 52: Robert M. Utley, *Frontier Regulars: The United States Army and the Indian, 1866–1891* (New York: Macmillan, 1973), 315; McWhorter, *Hear Me*, 553–89; Alan P. and Barbara Merriam, *Flathead Indian Music* (Missoula: Montana State University School of Music, 1950), 80; Gunther, "Western Movement," 180; Spinden, *Nez Perce Indians*, 226. O. O. Howard's writings, including his *Report to the Secretary of War* (Executive Documents, 45th Cong. sess. 2 [Washington, D.C.: Government Printing Office, 1877–78]), 606, are claimed by some to be more of a defense for the general's failure to bring the conflict to a quick close than a true assessment of Nez Perce tactics; nevertheless, his statements seem consistent with other, independent assessments.

14. Ray, "Ethnohistory," 110; *Cultural Relations*, 66.

15. Irving, *Adventures of Captain Bonneville*, 106, 107.

16. See Wayne Suttles, "Plateau Pacifism Reconsidered—Ethnography, Ethnology, and Ethnohistory," *Coast Salish Essays* (Seattle: University of Washington Press, 1987), 282–86. References to incidents of pacifism in the literature are rare compared to statements regarding the esteem associated with warriors. John A. Ross ("Political Conflict on the Colville Reservation," *Northwest Anthropological Research Notes* 2, no. 1 [1968], p. 56) presents an interesting viewpoint on the subject of presumed Plateau pacifism. Indians who followed their aboriginal faith, he writes, and who resisted encroachments by whites through diplomacy as well as belligerence, considered themselves much less pacifistic than their Christianized tribesmen who meekly turned the other cheek, allowing whites to take their lands, their culture, and their pride. As for Bonneville's frustration with the horseless Flatheads and Nez Perce, Thomas Leforge explained that dashing off in quest of quick vengeance was not the Indian way. They would "slip out on this kind of enterprise without informing anybody. They were influenced, too, by their 'medicine,' by the weather conditions, by superstitions of numerous kinds that no white man ever could comprehend"; Thomas B. Marquis, *Memoirs of a White Crow Indian* (Lincoln: University of Nebraska Press, 1974), 215.

17. *The Real People: Legend of the Stick Game* (Spokane: KSPS Television, 1976).

18. Grace Bartlett, in *The Wallowa Country, 1867–1877* (Fairfield: Galleon, 1984), cites up to fifteen parleys, councils, and confrontations between just the Wallowa band of Nez Perce and whites where Native diplomacy and restraint postponed violence.

"They Had Not Done Wrong To Be So Killed"

The Nez Perce War of 1877

In the years following the 1855 treaty, which established supposed Nez Perce sovereignty over a specified amount of land, public outcry for additional land provided politicians with perceived justification to wrest more land from this previously specified amount. A second treaty, then, had to be presented to the Nez Perce in 1863. The size of the Nez Perce reservation was to be reduced by nearly 80 percent. Chief James Lawyer and specially selected leaders of those Nez Perce who were already committed to living a somewhat acculturated reservation life signed this new treaty, ceding lands including the Wallowa valley, the country of Joseph's people, and the Salmon River country, that of Chief White Bird's people, to the whites, thus infuriating those Nez Perce leaders who chose not to sign. Lawyer already had his reservation established by the earlier 1855 treaty. Neither he nor any of his subchiefs had authority in the Nez Perce political system to sign away lands under the control of other chiefs.

Land which the Nez Perce depended on for subsistence and sustaining their basis of wealth, grazing land for their immense horse herds, was already being steadily encroached upon by settlers. Whites were even pouring into the established reservation in search of gold, and towns sprung up to serve and reap profits from the miners. On the reservation the new town of Lewiston continued to grow until the whites felt it had to be ceded, along with the Wallowa valley and Salmon River country. Though no gold in any quantity to impress anyone was reported to be found in the land claimed by Wallowa Nez Perce, white ranchers had their eyes on the lush natural pastures in the Wallowa, Grand Ronde, and Imnaha valleys. With the purpose of preserving their way of life, the Nez Perce sought ways to keep the peace and to stay near their beloved homeland. The father of young Chief Joseph erected a line of ten-foot peeled wooden poles secured with piles of rocks at their bases, to prevent white travelers and settlers from wandering by mistake or on purpose off the established wagon road and onto lands claimed by his band of Nez Perce.[1] The poles had little effect. Whites continued to encroach on Nez Perce land.

The "nontreaty" Nez Perce, as those who rejected this treaty came to be called, refused to comply with its directives. This refusal brought about a series of councils and meetings with agency, state, and military officials to clarify the terms of the new treaty, or to diffuse and placate difficult situations as they arose. Articulate and politically astute young Joseph was pushed to the forefront of negotiations, making appeals to military and agency representatives, trying desperately to maintain control of his land and way of life.[2] Joseph and his colleagues presented government officials with a list of strategies designed to defuse the tensions: sell parcels of Wallowa land to whites already settled there; divide the valley in half so it could be shared with the whites; or give up the valley completely and move in with their linguistic relatives, the Umitillas. Each suggestion involved an unwanted concession of land, freedom, and status. None of the councils or meetings made significant headway. Neither party came away pleased. The whites wanted the land; the Nez Perce did not want to give it up. Whites' and Indians' concepts of land-ownership were hopelessly at odds.

General Oliver Otis Howard, recently appointed head of the U.S. military's Department of the Columbia, was charged with aiding Nez Perce Indian Agent John B. Monteith in solving these problems. He was called upon by Agent Monteith to meet with the Nez Perce and "bring the Indians to terms," as the government put it—that is, to force them onto the reduced reservation if need be.[3]

The military garrison at Fort Lapwai was mobi-lized for action. The stage was being set for what became known as the third Lapwai council—yet another meeting between government representatives and the nontreaty Nez Perce. From Howard's and Monteith's viewpoint, it seems, the word "council" meant "Let's meet and tell these Indians what to do," more so than "Let's discuss the issues and reach a consensus."[4] A similar attitude may have been held by the Nez Perce, who came to the council prepared to defend their right to remain on their homeland. This council was the government's last effort to avoid a war yet achieve the goal of crowding all Nez Perce—ʔipnu' cililpt followers, Christians, buffalo hunters, salmon fishers, and farmers—onto the reduced Nez Perce reservation.

At first the chiefs were firm. None spoke in favor of leaving their homeland. Toohoolhoolzote, a leader in the ʔipnu' cililpt faith and chief of the small but influential Pikunan band living between the Snake and Salmon Rivers, chose to stand up to Howard's tough talk. Toohoolhoolzote's part in this council is described more often as a clash with Howard than as a speech. Frustrated and embarrassed, Howard finally felt the need for a show of force. He ordered Toohoolhoolzote to be arrested and locked up in the garrison jail.[5] Of this incident, of Howard's tough talk, and of the reinforcements called up from Fort Vancouver, Yellow Wolf, a Nez Perce veteran of the 1877 war, remarked, "In peace councils, force must not be talked. It was the same as showing us the rifle. That was what brought war, the arrest of this chief and showing us the rifle!"[6] Yellow Wolf's dismay at Howard's tough stance is understandable in this light.

Though Joseph said he would not leave his homeland till "compelled to," rumors of more troops on the way to the council grounds helped confirm this decision to go to the reservation.[7] Joseph's younger brother, Ollokot, not wanting to leave his wife and children alone while he fought the whites, also advocated the move to the Lapwai reserve. Finally, still attempting to avoid war, the nontreaty bands of Nez Perce decided to accept lands on the established Lapwai reservation according to Howard and Monteith's demands. "The chiefs were not talking war," explained Yellow Wolf. It was the young men who were talking of fighting. Always, the chiefs, even Lookingglass, one of the most noted warriors among them, warned that armed resistance against the whites was hopeless. "The power of the whites was such that all the chiefs believed there was no real hope of gaining their ends by fighting." So Nez Perce leaders gave orders, "Everyone get ready to move to our new home."[8]

Realizing the risks and potential futility of war, leaders of the nontreaty Nez Perce were in the process of moving their bands to the Lapwai reservation. Emotions ran high. Knowing a change in lifestyle was coming but not fully realizing how much of a change; being forced to move onto the reservation and having to share limited space with their acculturated relatives, the treaty/Christian Nez Perce; and having to make the move within the short period of thirty days—all made for a volatile situation.

A combined group of people from Joseph's and White Bird's bands were camped at a place called Tepahlewam, making preparations for their move to the reservation. Livestock had to be gathered and roots needed to be dried for future food stores. As often happened when a large group of Nez Perce got together, the warrior leaders and their followers took the opportunity to show off. They staged a parade around the camp. Showing off meant wearing the trappings of a warrior—weapons, shields, feather headdresses, and paint on both men and horses. The parade was probably even more important at this

camp than usual, the warriors desiring to show that their spirit had not been forfeited along with their land. Several variations of the story occur at this point but the principal character was a younger warrior named Walaytic. He and a friend, Sapsis ʔilpilp, took a position of honor bringing up the rear of the parade. Others in the camp taunted Walaytic. Here he was, they said, pretending to be a warrior, parading with the warriors, indeed, occupying one of the places reserved for the elite of the warriors, the rear guard, when all the while allowing the white man who murdered his father to live, unavenged, only a few miles from this very camp! The taunt was too much to take. Walaytic recruited his friend Sapsis ʔilpilp and a youth, Wetyetmes Weheyqt, to accompany him on his mission of vengeance. The trio never did make contact with the murderer of Walaytic's father, but other whites encountered by these three, and a subsequent group of raiders, were killed or wounded. Accounts of the number of victims vary. The low estimate is fourteen; the high, twenty-two.[9]

Returning to camp, the young warriors boasted about their exploits. The news caused excitement and concern. Recalling the zeal which the whites showed for punishing Indians, as evidenced during the 1848 Cayuse war and Wright's campaign against the Spokanes and Palouses in 1858, the chiefs knew that retaliation from the U.S. military was imminent.[10] Lessons learned during times of danger, while out on the bison plains, about strength in numbers and unity of purpose convinced the headmen that the assembled bands should stick together instead of turning Walaytic and his cohorts over to the authorities. The Nez Perce camp mobilized for defense. During this crisis, tribal unity gained such importance that Joseph and his followers, still hoping for a peaceful resolution to the crisis, were watched lest they try to disassociate themselves from the now hostile Nez Perce and flee to the Lapwai reserve.[11] Joseph was said to be considering ways, such as negotiating possible surrender of the killers, to keep his Wallowa people out of war.[12]

The hostiles, as nontreaty bands were now called, moved camp to White Bird canyon, a position more secluded than the Tepahlewam site. True, defense was important but the chiefs still held out hope for peace. After all, many Nez Perce considered the Salmon River raids justified revenge for previous wrongs, not the start of a new round of hostilities. But to the outraged whites, it was an act of Indian treachery, an act of war. Early on the morning of June 17, lookouts alerted the camp to the presence of a military force. Captains David Perry and Joel Trimble, under the command of General Howard, had discovered the Nez Perce and positioned their men for an early morning charge. Instead of confronting the expected Indian line of defense, the soldiers met a truce team from the camp. Before any serious negotiations could take place, members of a volunteer force accompanying the military opened fire on the truce team. The early bravado of the volunteers, however, waned quickly as the Nez Perce returned fire. Mounted warriors routed both the volunteers and the regulars. Military losses included a humiliating one-third of Perry's command plus numerous rifles, pistols, and cartridge belts which were picked up by the Indian warriors as spoils from fallen or panicked soldiers. An added prize was the acquisition of some of the soldiers' horses left by the fleeing troops.

It was a victory for the Nez Perce. The whites, they thought, had been taught a lesson. Maybe now the soldiers would leave them alone. Maybe a chance was still left that the Nez Perce could negotiate a peace, could live in or near their traditional homeland.[13] De-ciding to remain in the vicinity, the Nez Perce withdrew from White Bird canyon, looking for another defensible place to wait for future developments.

But the plans of the military could not be thwarted. Even though Lookingglass's people had not been involved in the Salmon River raids, Howard viewed them with suspicion. In an attempt to subdue what he thought would be a potential troublemaker, Howard ordered Captain Stephen Whipple to Lookingglass's camp with orders to arrest the chief. Rifle shots from Whipple's scouts interrupted a parley between the officer and representatives from the Nez Perce camp, killing or wounding several warriors. Not expecting trouble, Lookingglass's people were unprepared for a fight. They fled their camp, leaving behind most of their possessions including a large portion of their valuable horse herd. The frustrated and angry Lookingglass band, along with their close allies, a band of Palouses under headman Husus Kute, eventually found and joined the other hostiles, adding 160 warriors to Joseph's and White Bird's bands.[14]

Several encounters with the military occurred between July 4 and 10, including a disastrous engagement for Lieutenant Rains and skirmishes with soldiers and volunteers in the vicinity of Cottonwood, Idaho.

The Nez Perce were moving into the Clearwater River drainage country, tying to avoid the military yet stay near home territory. It was in these parts that Edward McConville and eighty volunteers came across their trail. When fired upon by Nez Perce sharpshooters, McConville and his volunteers retreated to the top of a knoll, there to be placed under siege for the remainder of the day and following night. The necessity of making a dry camp on their hilltop caused the frightened and wounded volunteers to spend a miserable night. The main goal of the Nez Perce, to halt the advance of the armed whites, being attained, the warriors turned to a second goal, the capture of McConville's horses. This they easily achieved since the volunteers were cowering atop their little hill waiting for the same fate, so they imagined, that Custer had met the previous year. Of the forty or so horses captured from McConville's volunteers, most were said to be ones "procured" by the whites from the fleeing Looking-glass band only eight days earlier.[15]

Up to this point, the Nez Perce had not fared badly in their contests with the military, and had gone into camp on the Clearwater River assuming Howard was back nursing McConville's volunteers on what became known as "Misery Hill." Howard, however, discovered the location of the Clearwater camp and made his attack. The Nez Perce were not necessarily surprised by the presence of troops, but were unprepared for Howard's attack.

Ɂiceyeye Pewwetes, one of the Nez Perce scouts, charged into camp reporting the advance of Howard's troops, but the first indication of an actual attack was the explosion near camp of shells from the general's howitzers. Howard's hoped-for element of surprise and his mounted charge toward the camp were quickly checked by Nez Perce sharpshooters. Soon Howard's troops were in retreat, seeking shelter from mounted warriors. While the soldiers were being pinned down on a grassy hillside devoid of much cover, a small band of warriors attacked Howard's pack train, killing at least two packers. Though the battle is generally viewed as a defeat for the U.S. troops, the truth of the situation had to be faced by the Nez Perce. Howard's soldiers meant business.

As poor as the soldiers' fighting ability seemed to be, the Nez Perce were convinced that these Idaho troops were intent on pursuing until the Indians were captured or annihilated. A council of chiefs made the decision to depart from the Idaho country and seek a new homeland on the Great Plains. They would leave these angry, spiteful soldiers behind and move to the bison country. With only four of their warriors killed in this battle but eighty lodges and lodge poles lost, the Nez Perce made a fast but relatively safe getaway from the Clearwater area.

Several more skirmishes occurred throughout July en route to the Montana plains. Though none could be called military defeats for the Nez Perce, the bad news was the lack of support, in fact outright hostility, exhibited by their former allies, the Flathead. One confrontation, with men under the command of Captain Charles C. Rawn, left some of the Nez Perce with the impression that they had made a peace treaty with the people and soldiers of Montana.[16]

Feeling safe, the Nez Perce went into camp beside the willows bordering the north fork of the Big Hole River. New tipi poles needed to be cut, clothing and gear required repair, and since Howard and his "Idaho soldiers" were left behind, the Nez Perce allowed themselves a badly needed rest. "It was almost a festive occasion," a relief from the tension of hostilities. A warrior's parade around the camp, similar to that fateful parade at Tepahlewam, was staged the next evening.[17]

In the early dawn of August 9, still at the Big Hole camp, an elderly Nez Perce rode out to check on his horses. He plodded across the Big Hole River, hesitated, and peered into the brush, his curiosity aroused by some unnatural silhouettes. He was immediately shot dead by soldiers of Colonel John Gibbon's command who were concealed in the thickets along the river. The identity of this man varies according to the source. Yellow Wolf claims it was Natalekin, and Trafzer and Scheuerman implicate the Palouse chief, Hahtalekin, for this early morning incident.[18] McWhorter claims Hahtalekin was the first to leave camp but quickly returned to report hearing soldiers whispering in the brush. It was old Wetisto Kaith, McWhorter writes, who went to look after his horses and was killed.[19]

Whoever this unfortunate individual was, the shots that took his life signaled the soldiers' charge into the still sleeping camp. Some of Gibbon's troops gained possession of the upriver end of the camp, fighting right among the tipis. Finally the Nez Perce warriors rallied and repulsed the troops. While the women tried to strike camp, the warriors held off the soldiers. The Nez Perce did make their escape but losses were heavy. Many remaining lodge covers, those not lost on the Clearwater, were left still draped around their poles at the camp. Walaytic and Sapsis ʔilpilp were both killed, as were other noted warriors. The Nez Perce lost not only their homeland, but now, they realized, even the safety of the Montana plains. A second rude shock followed the Big Hole disaster. Expecting to find allies and refuge among their former friends, the Crows, the Nez Perce received only more confrontation. Many of the Crows "affected to array themselves against the Nez Percés, but in reality their warlike operations were restricted to the capture of ponies,"[20] an attitude which was no comfort to the fleeing Nez Perce. Only one choice seemed left. Flight to Canada. Sitting Bull and his Lakota had fled there after experiencing the same harassment from U.S. troops. They would understand the Nez Perce's plight. The Lakota, it was hoped, would take in the Nez Perce refugees.

Skirmishes and engagements continued with the U.S. military along the way: at Camas Meadows with Howard's troops; with Sturgis in the upper Yellowstone Valley and at Canyon Creek; and with Moelchert and Ilges at Cow Island.

Again, badly in need of food and rest, the Nez Perce camped at the foot of the Bear Paw Mountains. White Bird claims that scouts were sent out only toward the rear, the chiefs not expecting troops to approach and attack from another direction. Having no food in camp and finding bison nearby, the war leaders decided that this was the time to make a camp and replenish the food supply before moving on to Canada.[21] But again it was a fateful pause. Colonel Nelson Miles and his troops, riding hard from the lower Yellowstone River, laid siege to the Nez Perce camp and finally forced them to terms of surrender on October 5. Joseph, as civil chief, pitying the suffering of the women, children, and wounded, surrendered to Miles. He and about four hundred Nez Perce were eventually transported to Indian Territory, and were not allowed to return to the Northwest until 1885. The actual number of those Nez Perce who surrendered varies according to the source consulted. McWhorter's estimate of 418 is considered close to accurate.[22]

Most historians end their accounts here, ignoring the successes and sufferings of those who escaped Miles's siege of the Nez Perce camp and continued on to Canada. The story of those who continued the flight is, in fact, an Indian story, few whites being on any part of the scene to record events of the refugees. Though an accurate count is probably impossible to obtain, it is said that over two hundred of the Nez Perce refused to surrender and fled from the Bear Paw battlefield. Several sources state that only one hundred escaped the Bear Paw battlefield, though this appears to reflect the number of refugees who survived the flight and finally encamped with Sitting Bull's Lakota.[23]

Some of the escapees were away from the main camp tending the horses or hunting bison when Miles attacked. These took advantage of their situation, using the horses as their means of escape. Others fled the camp, on foot, at various times through-out the siege, fighting their way through the troops in hopes of reaching Canada. Another group escaped with White Bird the night before Joseph formally surrendered to Miles. Whatever the circumstances of their escape, most left with only what they wore or could carry, unable to pack any of the remaining stores of food or supplies. Of these two hundred or so, some were recaptured by the military. Some died of injuries, hunger, or exposure before reaching Canada. Some were killed by other unsympathetic tribes. But some did manage to reach the safety of Canada, the Grandmother's land. Destitute and hungry, groups of Nez Perce refugees fortunately fell in with roving half-breed bison hunters of White and Cree ancestry. These Milk River Half-Breeds, as they were known, took pity on the straggling Nez Perce bands, fed and clothed them, and escorted or directed them to Sitting Bull's camp near Fort Walsh in Saskatchewan. The Nez Perce's identifica-tion of these friendly Indians or half-breeds varies in their accounts from "Chippewas" to "Crees" to "half-breeds."[24]

Although the Nez Perce and Lakota had a tradi-tion as enemies, the Lakota were outraged when they heard of the treatment the Nez Perce had received from the whites.[25] Nothing had changed since the previous year when the Lakota had been forced to flee the United States. The whites wanted Indian land and would stop at nothing to get it.

Yellow Wolf experienced some apprehension upon reaching the Lakota camp. The Lakota evidently were showing caution at accepting these refugees. Yellow Wolf told of his feelings: "I knew we never were friends to the Sioux [Lakota] Indians and it must mean they meant to kill us. This I well under-stood, and I had my rifle ready."[26] Another source,

however, claims the Lakota "were jubilant over the arrival of the Nez Perce."[27]

The Nez Perce apparently got along well with their Lakota hosts despite language differences. In 1879, Canadian Mounties had to deal with the mis-behavior of an allied Lakota and Nez Perce raiding party. James Walsh of the North-West Mounted Police was in charge of overseeing the behavior of the refugee Lakota. Walsh wrote that food was plentiful, bison roaming "in droves of thousands." In fact, he states that the Lakota claimed the span of 1877 to 1879 to be the "happiest days of their lives."[28] As usual, there are some conflicting reports com-plaining that the first winter in Canada was a lean one. Bison were scarce, some said, and Lakota sym-pathy could not fill the stomachs of the Nez Perce refugees.[29] Homesickness coupled with a fictitious story that Joseph had ordered the refugees to re-turn to Lapwai induced many to begin the journey "home" to Lapwai in June 1878.[30] Sporadic groups of returning Nez Perce drifted in to the reservation throughout the summer of 1878 and for the next four years. A few Nez Perce never returned to the Northwest, choosing to live with the Lakota. In an interview at the Squamish Pow Wow, North Vic-toria, British Columbia, Mrs. Lelah Stevenson told of how her great-grandmother fled to Canada from the Bear Paw battlefield and chose to stay with the Lakota. Mrs. Stevenson's mother's last place of resi-dence was South Dakota, where she lived with her Lakota husband, yet she still took pride in her Nez Perce ancestry.[31]

Those warriors who came back to Lapwai while Agent Monteith still reigned were turned over to military authorities and sent to Indian Territory with the other captives. Monteith's term as agent ended in 1879. Charles D. Warner was then appointed to replace him. Warner was the agent credited with a benevolent attitude that allowed successive refugees returning from Canada to remain on the Lapwai reserve.[32] It was under these more tolerant conditions that the *Cash Book* chronicle of the Nez Perce war was probably produced.

Notes

Chapter title quotation: L. V. McWhorter Papers, cage 55, folder 170, "Narrative Mrs. Ollocut," n.d., Washington State University Libraries, Pullman.

1. Lavender, *Let Me Be Free*, 192; Bartlett, *Wallowa Country*, 13.

2. White Bird, in a speech given to the North-West Mounted Police at Fort Walsh, Saskatchewan, seems to have felt he deserved the credit for advising and urging Joseph to council with the whites to maintain possession of the disputed lands instead of going to war, or instead of simply giving up and moving to the reservation. In this speech, White Bird claimed to have worked closely with Joseph during the months prior to the outbreak of hostilities. James Walsh to Cora Walsh, 1890, Glenbow Museum Archives, Calgary, Alberta, D 364.971 W 225.

3. Josephy, *Chief Joseph's People and Their War*, 4.

4. O. O. Howard, *Nez Perce Joseph* (Boston: Lee and Shepard, 1881), 64–66.

5. Nearly every account of the Nez Perce war relates what took place at this May 3rd Lapwai council. Comparison can be made between McWhorter, *Hear Me*, 159–68, who writes as an advocate for the Indian point of view, and Garret B. Hunt, *Indian Wars of the Indian Empire* (Spokane: Spokane Community College Library, n.d.), 112–13, whose sympathies lie far more toward the views of whites at the time of the conflict. Interestingly, both writers use the same facts and the same intensity of conviction to support opposing viewpoints.

6. McWhorter, *Yellow Wolf*, 41. Also see Duncan McDonald, "The Nez Perces," in Linwood Laughy, comp., *In Pursuit of the Nez Perce*, 234, 243.

7. Lavender, *Let Me Be Free*, 232. The reinforcements likely were members of Lieutenant James Haughey's infantry from Fort Vancouver. See Brown, *Flight of the Nez Perce*, 81.

8. McWhorter, *Yellow Wolf*, 41–42. Also see Merrill D. Beal, *"I Will Fight No More Forever"* (Seattle: University of Washington Press, 1963), 46.

9. There was talk of war with the whites, even before the outbreak of hostilities—that is, before a few young Nez Perce began their acts of retribution. Unpunished wrongs against Nez Perce people included twenty-eight or more Nez Perce killed by whites between 1863 and 1877. McWhorter, *Hear Me*, 226.

10. Donald M. Hines, *Ghost Voices* (Issaquah: Great Eagle, 1992), 8; Robert H. Ruby and John A. Brown, *The Cayuse Indians* (Norman: University of Oklahoma Press, 1979), 144, 238. Duncan McDonald refers several times to Nez Perce fears of being hung as criminals if they surrendered or were captured. This fear persisted, McDonald claims, throughout the war (*Nez Perces*, 238, 242, 249, 270).

11. Hampton, *Children of Grace*, 4, 340; McWhorter, *Yellow Wolf*, 45. Joseph, giving in to the arguments offered by his fellow leaders, is reported to have finally said, "I can hardly go back [to Lapwai]. The white people will blame me, telling me that my young men have killed the white men." John D. McDermott, *Forlorn Hope* (Boise: Idaho State Historical Society, 1978), 12.

12. *Nez Perce Country* (Washington, D.C.: U.S. Department of the Interior, National Park Service, 1983), 123, 124.

13. Wilson, *From Where the Sun Now Stands*, 14.

14. Brown, *Flight of the Nez Perce*, 168.

15. Ibid., 186.

16. Brown, using quotes from Duncan McDonald (ibid., 221), explains the Nez Perce's misconception that once across the Idaho border into Montana they would no longer have to worry about a hostile military force pursuing them.

17. "Nez Perce Camp: Big Hole National Battlefield" (Yellowstone Library and Museum Association, 1977); McWhorter, *Yellow Wolf*, 110.

18. McWhorter, *Yellow Wolf*, 115; Clifford E. Trafzer and Richard D. Scheuerman, *Chief Joseph's Allies* (Sacramento: Sierra Oaks, 1987), 19.

19. McWhorter, *Hear Me*, 380.

20. Marquis, *Memoirs of a White Crow Indian*, 129. Though the degree of hostile actions taken by the Crows against the Nez Perce varies depending on the source consulted, it seems that the Crows selected the middle road as Marquis writes, taking the opportunity to increase their horse herds at Nez Perce expense without hotly engaging them in combat.

21. Walsh letter (see note 2 above), 29.

22. McWhorter, *Hear Me*, 499.

23. Stanley Vestal, *Sitting Bull: Champion of the Sioux* (Norman: University of Oklahoma Press, 1957), 214.

24. McWhorter, *Hear Me*, 509, 510, 511, 532. That these people who helped guide the Nez Perce to the Lakota camp were half-breeds, or Metis, not Crees or Chippewas proper, can be safely assumed considering that the Metis occupied the Wood Mountain/Cypress Hills area of Alberta and Saskatchewan, and that the Crees, especially, were not on good terms with the refugee Lakota; see John Peter Turner, *The North-West Mounted Police* (Ottawa: Edmond Cloutier/King's Printer, 1950), 1:331.

25. Joseph Manzione, *"I Am Looking to the North for My Life": Sitting Bull, 1876–1881* (Salt Lake City: University of Utah Press, 1991), 99–100.

26. McWhorter, *Yellow Wolf*, 234.

27. Walsh letter, 33.

28. Ibid., 13, 25. Other Mounted Police reports tell of several Nez Perce participating with Poundmaker's Cree warriors as late as 1885, confronting Canadian forces at Cut Bank Hill during the Northwest Rebellion; Turner, *North-West Mounted Police*, 2:179.

29. McWhorter, *Hear Me*, 516. Turner (1:461) reports that by the end of 1879 the Lakota were becoming increasingly destitute due to overhunting of the bison herds by the numerous Native groups in the area. Claims of lean times may have been made after the happy days of 1877 to 1879.

30. McWhorter, *Yellow Wolf*, 238; Manzione, *"I Am Looking,"* 12.

31. Lelah Stevenson, personal interview, 31 August 1991.

32. Beck, interview, 6 June 1992; McWhorter, *Hear Me*, 517; *Yellow Wolf*, 291.

Form, Organization, and Artistic Style of the Cash Book

The *Cash Book* artist's individual drawings give a wonderful historical and ethnographic account of life and events during the 1877 Nez Perce war. They allow us a glimpse not only into the past but into the mind of one of the participants in the war, showing which events he took part in and what incidents he felt were important, all influenced by his personality and cultural background. Some attention paid to the methods and media used to produce the drawings, and to the drawings' organization within the *Cash Book*, give added insight on the content and about the artist himself.

PAGINATION

Although the original book is not paginated, for convenience in analyzing and describing the book's contents, the first leaf facing the front endpaper will be called figure 3, with numbers continuing consecutively throughout the book so that the final page, figure 43, is followed by an insert and the rear endpaper. (The fifteen blank pages throughout the *Cash Book* are not reproduced here but are mentioned, in brackets, at the end of the text for the preceding figure.)[1]

At least three pages, or leaves, have several separate pictures drawn on them, and each of these multiple-picture pages contains drawings showing a thematic similarity; for example, the three drawings in figure 6 relate to aspects of the ?ipnu' cililpt faith. Drawings in figure 4 and on the rear endpaper (fig. 45) show the same consistency of theme. Because of this consistency, the drawings in figure 6, as well as those in figure 4 and on the rear endpaper, will be treated as one composition to ease in cataloging and describing the *Cash Book* artwork. The term *drawing*, then, refers to the entire composition on each notebook page rather than to separate motifs and images occupying the same picture plane.

CASH BOOK TEXT: HEADINGS

Written notations for several purposes occur throughout the leaves of the *Cash Book*. What seem to be headings, in India ink, referring to men, women, horses, and soldiers (see *Cash Book* figures 4, 10, 11, 12, 14, 16, 19, 21, 22, 26, 29, 35, 38, and 40) occur irregularly nearly from cover to cover. Some of these headings were written hastily enough that the still-wet ink on them transferred to the facing page as the leaves were turned to continue the writing throughout the book (figures 12 to 13, 14 to 15, 21 to 20 and 29 to 28). These circumstances give rise to the notion that certain of the headings were written in preparation for some accounting business, a task with which an agency "clerk" such as G. D. Fleming might be charged.

No obvious sequential order has yet been recognized for these headings. They are not alphabetical nor are they oriented to the binding in a way that indicates any organization. When the booklet is arranged so the headings appear right side up, the relation of the writing to the binding occurs in three out of the four possible positions. It is only when the booklet is horizontal, with the binding positioned at the top of the page being viewed, that no headings appear right side up. "Cash Book," the phrase that appears to be a title displayed on the front cover, has been written by the same person who wrote the other India ink headings.

The need for drawing surfaces to record events dealing with the 1877 Nez Perce war took precedence over the presumed accounting intent of the little notebook. Within the same time span in which the drawings were being produced, someone—the artist or an agency employee perhaps—supplemented the pictorial chronicle of the war with verbal notations, using a variety of media.[2]

TEXT: *CASH BOOK* CAPTIONS

Forty-three written notations apart from the prepared headings actually do relate to the drawings. Some of these notations are in India ink, others are done in red, blue, or black colored pencil. The writing is as intriguing as the drawings are dynamic. A comparison of writing styles indicates that whoever did the preparatory headings in India ink likely did at least some of the other writing. The style of the notations is not as ornate as the headings but shows enough similar characteristics to assume that it is from the same hand as the headings. It also appears that some of the original writing was retraced and/or copied (by the Indian artist possibly) in colored pencil, the writing style again being similar to the title of the book and the headings.

Some captions written in the *Cash Book* are in English, some in Nez Perce. Nez Perce words are mostly names of individuals, spelled phonetically. Spelling variations of repeatedly attempted words (the name llamnieenim Hooshoos has been spelled at least six different ways throughout the *Cash Book*) show that the writer was struggling to transfer the sounds of the Nez Perce language into written English. Even English words posed some difficulties, the writer putting down "Hosre" for Horse, "Josphe" for Joseph, and "Saman" for Salmon. The possibility that the artist himself did the writing, even as events of the war took place, has not been ruled out.[3] Fortunately, some writing obviously relates to the subject on whose page the writing appears or is adjacent to.

Sadly, not enough writing was included to fully explain the intent of each drawing.

MEDIA AND TECHNICAL SKILL

The small size of the book was not a limiting factor to the artist. His drawings include close-up portraits of people showing their individualistic dress and ornamentation, as well as nearly panoramic views giving an idea of the large number of subjects or of the surrounding landscape. Over two-thirds of the already small drawings have been elaborated with details and patterns intended as much for decoration as to aid the viewer in understanding the intended action. The technical skill and artistic expression demonstrated by the *Cash Book* artist are equal to the best work of his contemporaries from the Great Plains. John C. Ewers, a noted authority on Plains Indian painting, had a chance to view some of the drawings (figures 4, 7, 18, 20, 24, 26, 30, 32, and 40). Of the artist's ability he says, "I do think that the . . . drawings compare well with ones executed by Sioux and Cheyenne artists of that period for the most part. They are much more detailed and anatomically accurate than most Blackfeet works of the same period."[4]

In addition to overcoming the difficulties of drawing on a small picture plane, the artist's choices of drawing media were severely limited. Black, red, and blue colored bookkeeping pencils, and possibly wax crayon and graphite pencil, were the extent of his materials. Working creatively within this limitation rather than suffering from it, the artist distinguishes one from another in a series of like images by alternating the color of each image (figures 20 and 23). The result is more decorative than accurate but achieves the goal of differentiating one image from the next. Unlike the writing, none of the drawings shows use of India ink. Most of the *Cash Book*

pictures were begun with contour guidelines using a black colored pencil. The majority of drawings, on twenty-two out of twenty-nine pages, were filled in with flat colors. Some show layering of one color upon another to create a new color, thus expanding the limited palette (figures 18, 20, 28, 35, 40, 41, and 42), or show purposeful changes of pressure on the pencils to vary the value of the colors (front endpaper, figures 1, 20, and 45).

The artist's technical skill shows in his boldness and confidence when depicting his subjects. Only four drawings of the twenty-nine are incomplete (figures 5, 17, 39, and 42). Only a few show evidence of alteration or ill planning (figures 9, 12, 28, 32, and 34). Two have practice sketches or aborted themes evident in the background (figures 3 and 6).

The ability to draw accurately involves translating images either from memory or from life into two-dimensional shapes, and recording those shapes on a flat drawing surface. While some of this ability is inborn, becoming truly proficient at drawing involves training and practice. In the event that formal training is absent, a perceptive person can apply techniques observed in the work of other artists. Two interesting questions arise: where did the *Cash Book* artist get his experience, and are more of his drawings in existence? On this, Ewers comments: "I would say that your artist . . . has learned a great deal from white artists' methods of rendering realistically proportioned and detailed human and horse figures. [Figure] number 24 is especially remarkable in the portrayal of front-view human figures in carefully detailed clothing."[5] The *Cash Book* artist's horses are indeed much freer in interpretation than those typical of other Native artists. Rather than the conventionalized Plains style pictographic horses, which are nearly always drawn in profile running from right to left across the picture plane, the *Cash Book* horses face a variety of directions as they run, prance, paw, or stand at rest.

To evaluate the level of control the artist had over his materials in order to achieve a neat, refined presentation, the drawings were rated by comparing one to another. Indicators such as possible use of a straight edge, staying within his guidelines when filling in shapes with color, and attention to detail helped in determining the level of control the artist exhibited for each drawing. A simple scale of 0 to 3 aided in analyzing his craftsmanship: 0 representing a recognizable drawing but otherwise nearly out of control, and 3 representing a drawing that shows exceptional care. The majority of drawings, twenty-two out of twenty-nine, rated either a 2 or a 3 on this scale. Seven drawings were assigned to the 1 category, which seemed to exhibit a "just get it done and move on" attitude (figures 6, 17 23, 28, 34, 39, and 41), and no drawings fit the out of control category. Mood, or maybe energy level, seemed to have something to do with the placement of the controlled and not-so-controlled drawings between the covers of the booklet—that is, if the drawings were produced starting from the front endpaper and working toward the back as it appears they were. The neater drawings are clustered more toward the front of the book, where the larger number of portrait drawings are also located. Careful rendering of individuals in their finest regalia fits the mood of these portrait drawings. Toward the rear of the book are a higher percentage of action and combat scenes focusing more on *event* than on *individual*. The level of care taken with the action drawings goes down compared with those near the front. It is as if the artist became caught up in the very mood he was trying to impart. As his style of drawing changes, it indeed affects the viewer, conveying a sense of the energy and tension experienced during combat.

Five pages have unidentifiable scribbles across them which seem not connected to the content of the book (figures 2, 11, 15, 21, and 28).

Related to the artist's control of his media is his degree of accuracy in depicting figures, their outfits, equipment, and the lay of the land. As an eyewitness to the 1877 war who made his drawings within four years after it happened (in contrast to drawings done by another Nez Perce participant in the war, Piyopyo Talikt, who produced his works forty years after the conflict[6]), the *Cash Book* artist had events, regalia, and setting fresh in his memory. This clear recollection, especially of individuals, is apparently responsible for the high degree of precision in the details. Specifics of regalia and setting accurately link individuals with their feats or fate. Though a Nez Perce tribal art and clothing style had developed since the 1860s, each warrior had his own modifications that showed individuality in beadwork designs; face, body, and horse paint; choice of weapons; and of course personal medicine items. Differentiation of facial features, even physique, however, was not necessary to identify specific warriors if a prominent shield design, headdress, or design painted on the flanks of a horse could be used for this purpose.

Drawings in figures 4, 8, and 17 show horses in an unusual posture, with both right legs stepping forward, an action rather unnatural for a four-legged creature. What at first may appear to be the artist's mistake, however, may be yet another example of his accuracy. Experienced warriors would include a certain amount of pageantry and exhibitionism during parades, designed in part to delight and inspire onlookers. Nez Perce horsemen may have taught their horses a number of fancy gaits for parades, possibly similar to those modern horsemen call single-foot, rack, or pacing. All of those three gaits, for example, require a horse at some point to have either both right legs or both left legs off the ground at the same time. The *Cash Book* artist may have simply recorded such parading activity accurately.

COMPOSITIONAL ANALYSIS OF THE DRAWINGS

In his compositional techniques, the *Cash Book* artist seems to have solved a potential problem involving cross-cultural aesthetic and visual communication preferences. Consciously or unconsciously, he has combined what he knew of Native techniques (such as emphasis on regalia instead of facial features or physiology to identify individuals, and emphasis on pictures instead of written words to convey the message of place and action) with European techniques, like use of a variety of viewpoints and varied compositions, texture and pattern, suggestion of distance through perspective, and the inclusion of women as subjects. Thus viewers from both Nez Perce and white cultures can grasp the basic messages in his drawings. Opportunities for contact with white culture seemed plentiful. First Sergeant Michael McCarthy writes of White Bird's people, "The Indians, White Bird's Band, were raised around here and had lived and trafficked with the whites, who were nearly all storekeepers, for a good many years."[7] What was true of White Bird's people was apparently true of other nontreaty bands. Advertisements, product labels, and calendar art all could have provided visual information that influenced the *Cash Book* artist's work. Steven Shawley attributed the artist's representational skill to the Nez Perces' long association with whites.[8] Northwest history books are filled with accounts by explorers, traders, missionaries, military people, and settlers that tell of interacting with the Nez Perce.[9]

White missionaries and teachers may also have been part of the *Cash Book* artist's experience. Susan McBeth described how visual arts were used as part of the Christian education curriculum offered pupils during her 1873–77 tenure on the Nez Perce reservation: "Mrs. Spalding could draw somewhat, and often made use of this art in her teaching of Bible truth. The Nez Perces believed in pictures. . . . The Sunday-school picture papers have a great attraction for them. How carefully I find them stored away in the rafters of their little homes. They are so eager to see what the picture is, and the pleasure is great, to the people as well as to the children." Though McBeth ministered to and taught the Indians living on the reservation, members of the nontreaty bands "often came in among the Kamiahans" and undoubtedly saw pictorial works of the Christian missionaries and others.[10] These visitors may have included the *Cash Book* artist. His variety of compositional techniques and subjects, and the ease with which he used those techniques throughout the *Cash Book*, attest to his skill in observation and his proficiency as an artist.

Compositionally, the *Cash Book* drawings can be sorted into six categories for purposes of study. The largest, containing eleven of the twenty-nine compositions, could be called linear in arrangement of shapes. The subjects are arranged one behind the other to emphasize their movement or quantity (figures 2, 7, 8, 17, 22, 28, 32, 41, and 42). Next in frequency are six compositions arranged to focus attention on a central subject. In art school terminology, these six have one *center of attention*, with the remaining shapes or figures in the composition arranged to achieve some degree of visual balance (figures 4, 12, 14, 18, 26, and 40). Five drawings split their pages vertically, with subjects on the right side and on the left, but leave the center of the page vacant (figures 31, 36, 37, 39, and 45, the rear endpaper). Although the drawing in figure 26 has no *object* as the center of attention, the viewer's eye tends to focus on the place where the noses of the two horses meet. True to the three rules and purposes defining center of attention in the Euro-American, mainstream cultural sense, this drawing has (1) one place, (2) near the center, (3) which attracts the viewer's attention.

Figures 31, 36, and 37 are scenes showing combat between the two warring sides. The obvious way to emphasize the opposing sides is to draw them physically opposite each other on the picture plane.

Three drawings have elements scattered across the page, resulting in an undefined arrangement of space (figures 6, 34, and 35). Two drawings show strong vertical symmetry, the right and left halves close to mirror images (figures 5 and 24). Only two drawings have made incomplete use of the picture plane, blank space being left as if the picture were poorly visualized or planned (figures 21 and 30).

When evaluating the *Cash Book* artist's compositional skill, the greatest weight must be given to the intent of the drawings rather than to a Euro-American or art school ideal of fine art. The artist selected linear compositions to convey the energy and direction of a prancing horse herd and of charging buffalo. An unfortunate packer, the center of attention of one drawing, meets his death trapped between two warriors in a visually balanced composition. Duels between Nez Perce warriors and their enemies show clearly who belongs to which side. Vacant space was allowed to exist between the combatants. The *Cash Book* artist's decisions regarding composition were made for clarity of expression, to deliver a message or record events in the most convenient and understandable way. This rationale held true for other decisions he made regarding the images he produced.

DIRECTION OF ACTION

In conventional Plains Indian pictorial art, the direction of action is from right to left. Ten drawings from the *Cash Book* have action moving from right to left. The other nineteen drawings vary from showing no action at all to having the action converge toward the center of the page. Clearly, the *Cash Book* artist was attempting to show us *how* the action occurred rather than simply allowing himself to be influenced by tradition or convention.

ORIENTATION OF THE PICTURE PLANE TO THE BOOK BINDING

Curiously, the *Cash Book* artist has oriented his picture plane, the rectangular page, so that when drawing, the binding was toward the bottom of the picture on well over half of the drawings. The remainder of them have the binding oriented either to the right or the left, but never toward the top. It may be more than coincidence that this same relationship of right-side-up production to orientation of the binding holds true for the India ink headings as well as for the drawings. This could be yet another argument for the artist himself being the original possessor of the book. Any discomfort the binding may have presented, as the artist's hand bumped over it, must have been offset by the advantage of having the lower leaves and cover of the book as a hand rest.

PERSPECTIVE

Distance and perspective are shown by several techniques common to artists of this genre. Overlapping forms, objects placed higher on the picture plane, and use of diminishing sizes establish relationships between objects to give the illusion of distance. Foreshortening, however, is a perspective technique not easy to apply without specialized training or a perceptive and analytical mind. Figure 4 shows a spirit horse prancing on a sun-disk. The disk is foreshortened, drawn as an oval to show how it is lying flat under the feet of the horse.

Although chiaroscuro shading to suggest three-dimensional form is all but absent, a value change from dark to light indicates the shaggy manes of the bison drawn in figures 2 and 20. Most of the horses, but notably those in figures 14 and 26, have a change in the thickness of their outlines which may be a device to imply shadow or form.

SCOPE AND VIEWPOINT

The scope or viewpoint in which the artist presents his subjects varies according to the action he tries to communicate. There is virtually nothing that could be called a close-up, and only four drawings emphasize a single important character on the picture plane (figures 4, 12, 14, and 30). Most drawings show multiple characters. On the other hand, there are three drawings, though not quite panoramic in scope, which show more distant views and include several subjects as well as simplified landscape features to help establish the physical setting for the action (figures 18, 34, and 35).

SEQUENCING OF THEMES

Though the *Cash Book* drawings may have been produced sequentially from the front to the back of the book, they do not read chronologically. There seems, however, a method to their organization for they have been arranged in groups according to theme. Figures 4, 5, and 6 comprise religious themes showing aspects of the ʔipnu' cililpt faith. Drawings probably intended as portraits are found near the front of the book also. Those in figures 8, 9, 12, 14, and 17, and possibly even 24 and 32, are of individuals or groups who may all be participants or spectators at a warriors' parade around the camp. Background embellishments have been left out so that the artist's energy and the viewer's attention could be focused on the individuals featured in these drawings. Scenes from the refugees' experiences in Canada appear next, using figures 18, 20, 21, and 26. Action scenes are grouped more toward the rear of the book, not beginning until figure 28 and continuing, interspersed between blank pages, to the end of the book. The action scenes are subdivided to feature significant events: pictures of two of the Three Red Coats at the Big Hole battle (figures 31 and possibly 30), the fight with Gibbon's soldiers among the tipis also at the Big Hole (figures 37 and 39), and finally the attack on Howard's packers and pack train on the Clearwater (figures 41, 42, and possibly 40).

MOTIVATION AND INTENT

Though the artist was at least as skilled as his Plains counterparts in freedom of expression, choice of subject matter, use of perspective, and depiction of action, his intent shows some departure from conventionalized pictographic art. Pressures of white expansion and a disrupted way of life brought about changes in the reasons for producing Native art. The pictographic art in ledger books, or even pocket notebooks like the *Cash Book*, is considered by some to be an intermediate stage in Native art development, a transitional phase between older hide painting and more modern ethnic art—that is, art produced for nontribal audiences.[11] Feest distinguished between various stages of Native art according to the purpose it was to serve. "Tribal art" was, and is, produced to fill the material or cultural needs of a particular tribal or ethnic group, and includes items such as beaded moccasins, painted parfleches, and women's fringed dance shawls. "Ethnic art" is produced by a particular tribal or ethnic group but is intended for a broader audience. For example, the *Cash Book* drawings are certainly Nez Perce in their ethnic origin but the evidence suggests that they were intended to document events of the 1877 war for a wider audience.[12]

Motives behind much of what is called "ledger art" are explained by Furst and Furst: "Some artists turned to painting partly . . . to fix the past in some more tangible form than oral narrative and memory. The lined pages of hardbound ledger books became especially popular for recording, with pencil, crayons, paints, and inks, the remembered glories as well as the bitter new realities."[13]

Unlike traditional hide paintings, the drawings of the *Cash Book* artist went beyond advertising successful war exploits. They portray themes rarely seen in ledger art. Subjects in the *Cash Book* include portraits, women, camp scenes, ceremonial dances, and abstract themes such as depictions of the artist's religion. The fact may well be that the term "pictographic art" as it is associated with conventionalized nineteenth-century Native art should not apply to the *Cash Book* drawings.

All of these topics presented in the *Cash Book* are tied into the fact and legend of the Nez Perce way of life and the 1877 war. Being from a people whose tribal history is kept largely in the oral tradition, the *Cash Book* artist must have felt that these events needed a more permanent, visual record. The importance of recalling tribal history is explained in the opening remarks printed in the Chief Joseph and Warriors Memorial Celebration program: "We, the members of the Chief Joseph and Warriors Memorial Celebration Committee, support and promote the cultural traditions that accord honor and respect to those Nez Perce who sought peacefully then fought honorably in war to survive and protect the lands, homes, graves, and beliefs of their forefathers for their children."[14] During the Saturday night portion of the Chief Joseph and Warriors Memorial Celebrations, honored Nez Perce, descendants of those who participated in the war, are called to the microphone to recount their ancestors' plights and tell their vision for the future. The importance of accurately recording those events is underscored by Yellow Wolf's comment to writer Lucullus McWhorter, who in collaboration with survivors of the 1877 war wrote the Indian side of its history: "The story will be for people who come after us. For them to see, to know what was done here. Reasons for the war, never before told. Nobody to help us tell our side—the whites told only one side."[15]

The *Cash Book* artist, along with Charles D. Warner and the Beck family, has ensured that an accurate and unique account of the Nez Perce people's involvement in that conflict will be available to "people who come after."

Notes

1. The Idaho State Historical Society, now in possession of the *Cash Book*, has photographed the book's pages and has assigned a number to each photograph. Except for the covers, Warner's inserted note, and blank pages, most photographs show two facing pages. So that attention can be focused on individual pages instead of pairs of facing pages, I have chosen to number each page sequentially.

2. An extensive search through the National Archives, Indian Office Records, and other institutional archives for the years 1881–82 has revealed no Lapwai Agency reports written in any hand comparable to the one in the *Cash Book*. Neither Charles Warner's, John Monteith's, nor

Charles Monteith's writing resembles the *Cash Book* script enough to claim that one of these men might have produced the writing.

3. Charles Geyer's footnotes to his "Notes on the Vegetation and General Character of the Missouri and Oregon Territories . . . 1843 and 1844" (*London Journal of Botany* 5:523) describe his observations of Henry Spalding's efforts at educating the Nez Perce in white ways: "The greater number read and write their own language well."

4. John C. Ewers to author, 22 January 1993. For detailed examinations of the characteristics of Plains pictorial art, refer to John C. Ewers, *Plains Indian Painting* (Palo Alto, CA: Stanford University Press, 1939), 17–20; Dorothy Dunn, *American Indian Painting* (Albuquerque: University of New Mexico, 1968), 153; Karen D. Petersen, *Plains Indian Art from Fort Marion* (Norman: University of Oklahoma Press, 1971), 21, 54; F. Dennis Lessard, "Plains Pictographic Art: A Source of Ethnographic Information," *American Indian Art*, Spring 1992, 62–69, 90; and David M. Fawcett and Lee A. Callander, *Native American Painting* (New York: Museum of the American Indian, 1982), 7.

5. Ewers to author, 22 January 1993.

6. Talikt's drawings are housed in the Holland Library Archives, Washington State University, Pullman. Piyopyo's name is spelled variously, McWhorter using "Peopeo Tholekt." Aoki's spelling, above, was selected for this text (see Harou Aoki, *Nez Perce Dictionary* [Berkeley: University of California Press, 1994], 1120). Several other Native artists have produced drawings of the 1877 war. These are discussed in Theodore Stern, Martin Schmitt, and Alphonse F. Halfmoon, "A Cayuse–Nez Perce Sketchbook," *Oregon Historical Quarterly* 81, no. 4 (Winter 1980): 346, and *Nez Perce Country*, 14–15.

7. McDermott, *Forlorn Hope*, 1.

8. Steven D. Shawley, telephone interview, 15 June 1992.

9. For a variety of examples of this Nez Perce–white contact from only one of the many sources, see Linwood Laughy, comp., *In Pursuit of the Nez Perces* (Wrangell, Alaska: Mountain Meadow Press, 1993), 9–11, 85, 216–17, 233–34, 248. Actually, hard evidence of white influence on the *Cash Book* art is difficult to find now. Early photographs of Lewiston, Enterprise, and other towns in Nez Perce territory indicate that most storefront and side-of-the-wagon advertisements consisted of lettering only, with an occasional scroll or calligraphic embellishment. Some product labels on canned, bagged, and boxed goods do have pictures accompanying the lettering, but most show easy to recognize profiles of the products, not action pictures or complex perspective techniques. Commenting on the absence of period calendars, magazines, and art prints in regional museums, a docent at the Asotin County Historical Society remarked, "They were very rough mining and lumber towns for the most part. I don't think people in those days had much use for fancy signs, magazines, or wallpapers" (personal interview, 20 July 1998).

10. In Kate McBeth, *The Nez Perces Since Lewis and Clark* (Moscow: University of Idaho Press, 1993), 44, 122, 90.

11. Dunn, *American Indian Painting*, 168; Petersen, *Plains Indian Art*, 70.

12. Christian Feest, *Native Arts of North America* (New York: Oxford University Press, 1980), 14–16.

13. Peter T. and Jill L. Furst, *North American Indian Art* (New York: Artpress, 1982), 168.

14. Chief Joseph and Warriors Memorial Celebration program (Lapwai: Chief Joseph and Warriors Memorial Celebration Committee, 1983), 2.

15. McWhorter, *Yellow Wolf*, 291.

"The Young Generation Behind Me,

For Them I Tell the Story"

The Cash Book Artist

A good many chroniclers, historians, and authors have made attempts to describe the events, terrain, participants, and emotions having to do with the 1877 war. The *Cash Book* drawings are one of exceptionally few sources that present images from the conflict, and not *just* images but those deemed important from the Indian standpoint, offering a Nez Perce version of the war.

ONE ARTIST OR MORE?

At the outset of my efforts to identify the *Cash Book* artist, there was some indication that the drawings might have been produced by more than one artist.[1] Two drawing styles are noticeable, roughly divided between the front or earlier pages and the rear or later pages (the parade or charge scene in figure 32 could be considered a turning point). This arouses speculation that more than one artist contributed to this book. These two drawing styles are characterized by:

1. A subject matter shift from the portraits, religious pictures, and Canadian scenes in the first three-quarters of the book to action scenes clustered in the last quarter

2. A change in viewpoint from close-ups and portraits, which occur more frequently in the front part of the book, to a more wide-angle approach, as one sees in the action pictures later in the book (this broader view of the scene, of course, helps the viewer better understand the setting of the action)

3. An apparently new medium, wax pencil or crayon, introduced into the later action and combat scenes, and especially noticeable in the drawings of the attack on the mule packers (figures 40, 41, and 42)

4. A method of color application in later drawings different from the method used in earlier drawings, involving more layering or mixing of red and blue or red and black
5. Black colored pencil outlines characteristic of earlier drawings are lacking in the later ones or have been replaced by blue pencil outlines (overall, the impression of these later combat scenes is one of more energy, of quickness of production)

The question of more than one artist is thus quite understandable. It can be resolved, however, by comparing similarities, rather than differences, between the later drawings and the earlier ones. Details such as the horses' fetlocks and hoofs, and the humans' facial features, show consistency throughout the book. A careful study of these details supports the case for a single artist who either tired as he approached the end of the book or experienced a mood change as he produced the action and combat drawings. Clinching this argument is the statement by Agent Charles Warner, written on a paper inserted into the *Cash Book*, saying that the drawings were done by "a Nez Perce Indian with Joseph war party" (see figure 44). Our conclusion is therefore that the *Cash Book* is the product of one artist with humanly different moods.

THE *CASH BOOK* ARTIST

A few things can be assumed with some degree of certainty. One is that the artist was male. Intimate knowledge of warriors, their accouterments, and of events on the field of battle are things to which a man would pay attention. Realistic pictorial art (beadwork aside) also falls within the male realm. Further, he was likely of warrior age—at least seventeen but not yet forty. He was apparently associated with, or

knowledgeable about, the younger generation of warriors. Many of the incidents he recorded and individuals' names placed like captions near certain drawings have to do with the exploits of youthful Nez Perce war participants. Warner's inserted notation confirms the artist's involvement in the war (though his statement fails to specify that the artist was a warrior). Also, the subject matter of the drawings is, for the most part, warrior-related, having to do with warrior parades or combat scenes. Some of the artist's experiences can be inferred from his drawings. He was likely a witness, maybe even a participant, in most of the incidents portrayed in the *Cash Book*. He certainly escaped from the Bear Paw battlegrounds and made his way to Canada to live for a while with Sitting Bull's Lakota. His stay in Canada must have lasted through the summer of 1878, long enough to witness at least one Lakota Sun Dance, these ceremonies normally being held in July "at the full moon of midsummer."[2] He returned to Lapwai, where he most likely produced the drawings, maybe for Superintendent of Farming G. D. Fleming.

A clue to the identity of the artist can be found in one of two sets of written notations in the *Cash Book*. The first set, as explained above, is made up of headings unrelated to the artist's work. Most of the second set of notations are names of individuals. One name, Laamnisnimusus, occurs ten times, with nearly as many spelling variations, throughout the booklet. The task, then, was to find a Nez Perce name compatible with these phonetic versions. Experts on the Nez Perce language were consulted to see if an agreement could be reached as to the meaning of this word. It was determined that Laʔamninnim Husus was closest to the pronunciation of the *Cash Book* spellings while retaining meaning in the Nez Perce language. In direct translation, llaminee or laʔam can mean "worn or withered away." Hooshoos translates as "head," but when preceded by "nim" it modifies "head" to the more general meaning "a part of one's body." When put together as a name, a translation could be "Skinny" or "Not much there of a whole body."[3]

That a man named Laamnisnimusus or Laʔamninnim Husus was the *Cash Book* artist seems a safe assumption. Considering the detail in the drawings, the artist knew his subjects well. He recorded incidents that were not well documented in other Nez Perce records, such as the assaults on Howard's mule packers and events in Canada, while leaving out incidents explained by other participants, for example Piyopyo Talikt's involvement in the attack on Howard's howitzer. Like that other chronicler of the Nez Perce war, Piyopyo Talikt, the *Cash Book* artist recorded events in which he was involved. It makes sense for the artist's name to recur in the *Cash Book*.

Laʔamninnim does not figure prominently either in known literature about the war or in the narratives of Piyopyo Talikt, Many Wounds, or Yellow Wolf, some of the most quoted Nez Perce participants in the war. As Yellow Wolf remarked to McWhorter, who sometimes questioned the old warrior to the point of frustration, "I never had no time in keeping track of everybody."[4] Yet with the name occurring ten times in this little booklet, Laʔamninnim Husus, artist or otherwise, acquires some importance in Nez Perce tribal history.

If indeed the artist is Laʔamninnim Husus, little is known about him. A summary of incidents and bits of information which help establish a correlation between Laʔamninnim Husus and the artistic production in the *Cash Book* also sheds a ray or two of light on who he may have been. Phonetic spellings of Laamnisnimusus appear more than any other name in the *Cash Book*, suggesting that the drawings

were largely about, and probably produced by, this individual.[5] He was probably a participant in the battles and survived to witness a Lakota Sun Dance, indicating that the artist's stay in Canada lasted longer than the documented return trip Yellow Wolf and his group of refugees made in June 1878.[6] Beyond that, Duncan McDonald, one of McWhorter's many informants, implicated a Charley llamnieenimhooshoos in the death of the Nez Perce chief, White Bird, during the exile in Canada.[7] During the Mounted Police's inquiry into White Bird's death, the testimony of a Nez Perce named No Feathers implicated "Tamnisuim Husus" as the assailant.[8]

The similarity of the name given by McDonald and No Feathers to that determined by those Nez Perce who reviewed the versions in the *Cash Book* may be coincidental. To accept a conclusion that McDonald's Charley llamnieenimhooshoos is the artist, or is the Laʔamninnim Husus of the *Cash Book*, would be irresponsible. Records of the North-West Mounted Police indicate that White Bird was killed in Canada in March of 1892, at least ten years after the *Cash Book* was produced. Additionally, White Bird's killer, documented as "Sam" or Charley Hasenahamahkikt on the arrest records, was captured and sent to Stony Mountain Penitentiary, Manitoba, to serve a life term for murder.[9] The arrest records also show that Hasenahamahkikt was about twenty-two years old when imprisoned for the killing. Looking backward in years to the 1877 conflict, Hasenahamahkikt would have been about eleven, not old enough to participate in the numerous combat scenes depicted in the *Cash Book* and hardly old enough to recall and record the amount of detail in the drawings.

Two possibilities emerge from these bits of information. First, Charley Hasenahamahkikt may have formerly been known as Charley llamnieenimhooshoos. Name changes were common among the Nez Perce. If so, his father or uncle may have had the same name, another practice not unknown to the Nez Perce, and could have been the Laʔamninnim Husus of the *Cash Book* text.[10] Considering the quality of the artwork, llamnieenimhooshoos the elder, if an elder llamnieenimhooshoos did exist, would be the candidate for its production. A second, more likely possibility is that McDonald may have received misinformation or may himself have been confused, mistakenly naming our presumed artist as the murderer llamnieenimhooshoos (or Laʔamninnim Husus), actually having no direct connection with the accused killer of White Bird. Laʔamninnim may simply have been a refugee-turned-artist. Since both possibilities are largely speculative, until more information about Laʔamninnim Husus surfaces some degree of uncertainty remains about who the *Cash Book* artist was. Even a production date and place of the drawings must remain ambiguous unless specific and reliable information surfaces. As to his fate, a brief report by Nez Perce war survivors Many Wounds and Black Eagle states that "La-am-mish-nim Hus-sus died in Montana."[11]

Notes

Chapter title quotation: Yellow Wolf to L. McWhorter, in McWhorter, *Yellow Wolf*, 18.

1. Candace S. Greene mentions cases where more than one artist contributed to the pictorial content of a ledger book. See "Artists in Blue: The Indian Scouts of Fort Reno and Fort Supply," *American Indian Art*, Winter 1992, 50–57. I was, in fact, encouraged by others to give serious consideration to this possibility (Ewers to author, 22 January 1993; Peters, personal interview, 19 June 1993).

2. Frances Densmore, *Teton Sioux Music*, Bureau of American Ethnology Bulletin 61 (Washington, D.C.: Government Printing Office, 1918), 98.

3. Letter from Kevin Peters, which included a response from Horace Axtell, 27 October 1993. Axtell and Peters suggested "llamnieenim Hooshoos" as a way to represent this individual's name in the English language. But to remain consistent with the spelling of other Nez Perce names in this work, Aoki's variation of "Laʔamninnim Husus" will be used. Richard Ellenwood pronounced the name "(i)Lamnis'inim' Hoos'hoos," suggesting "No Eyes" as a translation (personal interview, 7 August 1994). Aoki elaborates on laʔam, emphasizing verbs such as "exhausted" and "consumed," which could add even more variations to the translation of his name (*Nez Perce Dictionary*, 318–20, 1266).

4. Lucullus V. McWhorter Papers, cage 55, folder 520, Washington State University Libraries, Pullman.

5. Pictographic and ledger art frequently served a warrior's vanity through self-glorification. See Petersen, *Plains Indian Art*, 17 and 21; Dunn, *American Indian Painting*, 153; Ewers, *Plains Indian Painting*, 17.

6. McWhorter, *Yellow Wolf*, 238.

7. McWhorter, *Hear Me*, 524.

8. Photostatic copies of North-West Mounted Police records in possession of George Kush, reviewed 7 August 1994; *Alphabetical Inventory of Persons Sentenced to Death in Canada, 1867–1976* (1994, photostatic copy provided by Glenn Wright, Public Affairs and Information, Royal Canadian Mounted Police, correspondence of 16 January 1997), 238–39. Adding to the confusion, McDonald's name does not include the "s" sound in the first name, as do No Feathers's and the variations in the *Cash Book*. Given the similarity of the names and considering Ellenwood's pronunciation, McDonald probably misspelled or mispronounced the name. Still, care must be taken to avoid making definitive statements about the *Cash Book* artist.

9. McWhorter Papers, cage 55, folder 163, p. 49, "Killing of White Bird"; Kush interview, 7 August 1994. Several recent publications list the year of White Bird's death as 1882, which may be the result of Yellow Wolf's statement to McWhorter that the murder occurred "maybe about five years after the war" (Lucullus V. McWhorter Papers, cage 55, folder 163, "Yellow Wolf, July 1926. Anec-

dotes of Chief Peo Peo Hi Hi: 'White Bird.'" Photocopies of the North-West Mounted Police arrest and conviction records for this case, in the possession of Mr. Kush, are dated 1892.

10. Horace Axtell, personal interview, 7 August 1994. Even McWhorter occasionally faced confusion regarding an individual's name, writing, "The Indian proneness to multiple names precludes any clear identification" (*Hear Me*, 238).

11. McWhorter Papers, cage 55, folder 163, 1928, p. 13, "Nez Perces Who Escaped to Canada and Never Were Captured." Many Wounds and Black Eagle provide us with a spelling variation of this name amazingly close to one in the *Cash Book*. Compare their spelling, "La-am-mish-nim Hus-sus," with that on *Cash Book* page 51, "Laamnisnimusus." Tracking down this individual may be impossible. Not only did name changes take place in aboriginal culture, but many refugee Nez Perce were reported to have dropped their Indian names in favor of anglicized names to mask their previously hostile attitudes. This is entirely possible if the artist did move into Montana. Nancy Halfmoon and Dorothy Jackson, personal interviews, 15 August 1992. Also see McDermott, *Forlorn Hope*, 162.

A Presentation of
Nez Perce Ethnology and History
The Cash Book Drawings

*T*hree general themes guide this analysis of the individual pages of the *Cash Book*: (1) artistic materials and quality; (2) the presumed intent or historical significance of the words, people, and action pictured; and (3) the ethnological content of the drawings.

Artistic methods in general and specific ones pertaining to individual drawings are described as they relate to presumed intent—the message the artist apparently wished to communicate to the viewer. Many of the historical explanations of the drawings are guesswork, although it is guesswork guided by matching historic facts verified by other sources with the clues provided by the *Cash Book* artist. Explanations are heavily infused with qualifiers such as "may be," "possibly," and "likely" for the numerous instances of uncertainty in trying to match the action shown in the drawings with known individuals and events of the 1877 war. When appropriate, other interpretations and opinions are offered.

By far the most precise statements that can be made about the drawings have to do with their ethnological content. F. Dennis Lessard emphasizes the ethnohistorical importance of pictographic records such as the *Cash Book*: "Their real importance is as accurate historical records of Indians' views of themselves, their enemies, and their culture. Many drawings . . . give specific details of material culture —indeed, some recorded information that is found nowhere else."[1] The little *Cash Book* certainly provides a great deal of ethnographic information as well as offering much for speculation and further research. Just as important as the history and ethnology are the emotional responses the pictures evoke. The *Cash Book* artist has given us images that help us better understand the intermingling of camaraderie, resolve, and tragedy that is the story of the Nez Perce people and the 1877 war.

FIGURE I. FRONT COVER

"Every so often we'd get the book out and let the kids look at the Indian pictures."—Mary Beck

The "Indian book" that entertained Mrs. Beck's family is a 2³/₄ by 4⁵/₈ inch (7 by 12 centimeter) leather-covered booklet. The words "Cash Book," written in India ink, provide a title for the little book, typical of pocket notebooks available in stationery and mercantile stores of the late 1800s. Similar ones were said to have been issued to military personnel, especially junior officers, to keep track of orders and duties for the day.

A 1¹/₄ inch diameter (3 cm) circle pressed or inscribed into the leather of the front cover matches a circle on the back cover. Theories on the origin of the circles encompass a wide range of possibilities, but no single suggestion stands out as being primary.

FIGURE 2. FRONT ENDPAPER

"Wacamios, he was a buffalo hunter."
—Nancy Halfmoon

*T*wo running bison are drawn in black colored (not graphite) pencil. Certain areas have been colored darker to show the difference in texture between the bison's lighter shaggy mane and the rest of the body. Black pencil was used to write the word "Buffalo." Sketches of other bison parts are also perceptible on this page. To the right are blue outlines of a partial bison head. A black hoof or hoofprint is discernible near the center of the page. Other ill-defined marks in blue and red pencil occupy the background.

Wacamyos was one of the noted Nez Perce warriors who gained his combat experience while out on the Plains hunting buffalo (actually *Bison bison*). Trips across the Rocky Mountains to the bison grounds could last several months or more than a year. Not all Nez Perce bands made these hunting trips to the Plains. The upriver Nez Perce, those living generally on the Clearwater River drainage upstream from Lapwai Creek, were said to engage more regularly in bison hunts than their downriver relatives. The downriver bands, relying more on local fish and root resources, still enjoyed goods brought back from the Plains not only for their own use but to incorporate into their intertribal trade network. A wide range of products were obtained from these large beasts. Robes provided bedding and warm winter wraps, while dehaired hides were used for tipi covers and containers. Sinew was the craftworker's thread. Tough bison rawhide was necessary for shields, saddlery, and parfleches (rectangular storage cases), and lariats and bridles were sometimes made from braided bison hair. Dried bison meat added to the winter's store of preserved roots and fish; horns were made into utensils; and, of course, stories of the hunt and battle provided hours of entertainment while confirming a man's virility and status.

This drawing could simply be intended to proclaim the general usefulness and desirability of these animals. Drawings on the rear endpaper may make a similar statement about salmon. Those Nez Perce bands who hunted bison are reported to have felt themselves a bit superior, a bit more worldly than those who did not.[2]

On the other hand, this drawing may portray a particular incident. It is told that bison were being hunted by small parties during the opening attack at both the Big Hole battle and at the Bear Paws.[3] Red Elk lamented, "I heard the people talking afterwards had they not stopped to kill buffaloes they could have been across the (Canadian) border."[4] Even in exile, the Nez Perce and Lakota cooperated in hunts, targeting Canadian bison herds. The importance the *Cash Book* artist placed on specific events could qualify this drawing as an introductory scene to the battle on the Big Hole River or the final siege on Snake Creek in the Bear Paw Mountains. These two bison were soon-to-be camp meat, possibly pursued by the *Cash Book* artist or his comrades.

FIGURE 3

"How did they [the Indian artists] get the plentiful practice essential to the firm, disciplined hand . . . apparent?"
—Petersen, *Plains Indian Art from Fort Marion*

Barely perceptible on this first page of the *Cash Book* are line sketches in black pencil. One is of a human head with a large nose almost in caricature style. Another appears to be a bison hoof. Additional undefined marks also occupy this page. Arbitrary arrangement of these images could lead one to believe that this was a practice page instead 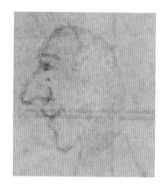 of an unfinished composition. This may answer, in part, the question of where this particular artist got his practice.

The word "Buffalo" appears again, this time written in blue pencil. Above "Buffalo" is another word, "teket." When the Nez Perce speak of bison hunting in their own language, they call the activity "tuk^{w}eyte." [5] These two words serve as a caption for the drawing of the two bison on the opposite page (figure 2, front endpaper).

[Followed in the *Cash Book* by three blank pages]

*T*he words "Horse" and "Sun" have been written in India ink and later retraced with red pencil. It is doubtful if the letter P, also in India ink, relates to the drawing. Outlines in black pencil define most of the shapes on the horse, disk, rainbow, and circular emblem at the upper left. Diagonal lines across the horse's body define powerful shoulder muscles.

This drawing, and those in figures 5 and 6, relate to aspects of the Ɂipnu cililpt faith. It seems the artist was asserting his association with the Ɂipnu cililpt or nontreaty Nez Perce. Even after his return to the Lapwai reservation, which supposedly required the renunciation of his native beliefs and acceptance of Christianity, he felt compelled to record images associated with the religion of many of his kinsmen who fought the government troops.[6]

These images include a horse prancing upon a six-rayed disk. The disk and horse are outlined by colored bands. A rainbow arches above the horse. Suspended from the arch of the rainbow are three bells. A bell also hangs from the horse's neck. Decorating the disk is a five-pointed star. The words "Hosre" [*sic*] and "Sun" indicate the principal subjects of this drawing.

It is doubtful that the *Cash Book* artist intended to hide the message or meaning of this drawing. The meaning is unintelligible only to those unfamiliar with native Nez Perce religion, for symbols and images familiar to the artist and his people are used here to communicate spiritual beliefs. Celestial objects including the rainbow, star, and sun-disk were central to the Ɂipnu cililpt faith, having connections with the heavens and the spiritual realm. The rainbow was recognized as having certain powers in itself. It could be seen but not grasped or captured. A rainbow's association with the earthshaking forces of thunder storms enhanced its power even more. Spiritual traits attributed to the rainbow were also practical traits valued by successful warriors.[7]

One corner of the page is decorated with a circle. It could easily be taken for a shield, but may instead be another emblem of the ?ipnu cililpt faith. Native people of the Northwest recognized spiritual attributes in many species of birds, including geese, meadowlarks, and orioles. One of the many services provided by certain birds was the ability to carry messages between the physical and spiritual worlds. Circles and disks were motifs connected directly with the Creator and the sun, the givers of life and light.[8] The combined design of bird and circle probably depicts a spiritual messenger and the Creator. This concept fits better with the larger spiritual theme of the page than does the depiction of a shield.

Hand bells played an important part in ?ipnu cililpt and reservation Christian church services. Both used hand bells to signal the call to worship as well as to indicate various stages of the worship service.[9] The sound of the bell, like the beat of a drum, was likened by some to a human heartbeat, the sound of life.[10]

Many motifs in this drawing appear in groups of three, a number which held sacred significance among those following ?ipnu cililpt beliefs—three bells, three bands on the rainbow, three feathers in the horse's forelock, three hoofprints each from the horse's front and rear feet. The number three occurs regularly throughout the recorded history and lore of the Plateau people. A dance for protection and good fortune was performed in three sets, thus ensuring its potency, by people of the middle Columbia; characters in legends and oral traditions jump over their deceased partners three times to bring them back to life; and when one wanted to fully assert himself, to swear an oath, he would include a phrase like "three times I tell you" in his statement.[11]

Portrayal of the horse as the major subject of this drawing emphasizes the importance of these animals to the Nez Perce people. Horses provided the primary method of transporting goods and people on

earth, why not a spirit horse for transporting the souls of temporarily deceased prophets to heaven, then back to earth bearing their prophecy?

The horse prances on a sun-disk, the disk being foreshortened into an oval to help show that the horse is physically on the disk. A well-documented part of the ?ipnu cililpt faith, the sun can be associated with things other than the Creator. In possible connection with the horse, the sun also was recognized as a method of transportation, carrying souls to their after-earth dwelling place; and along with other celestial bodies it was a symbol of life and was holy, since it shared the sky with heaven.[12] The sun and its symbolic motifs, the circle and disk, represented hope for renewal of the earth and a return to the traditional Native way of life as preached by the Washani leaders.[13] Two groups of three points or rays are apparent at the right and left arcs of the disk on which the horse is prancing. These rays can be variously interpreted as sun rays, points on a star, or even lightning.[14] Whichever is the accurate interpretation, all have to do with celestial powers, and the grouping of three is significant.

Stars, suns, and in fact most celestial bodies and phenomena, occupy a prominent place in ?ipnu cililpt beliefs. A look at the art and artifacts displayed in the collection housed in the Nez Perce National Historic Park museum (Spalding, Idaho) revealed at least five items decorated with star motifs using color schemes nearly identical to that depicted on the sun-disk of this drawing. Stars, it was said, acted as messengers to Lishwailait, an influential Plateau prophet associated with the Dreamer religion; and so important were the stars to Lishwailait that he had that motif appliquéd on his clothing.[15]

[Followed in the *Cash Book* by a blank page]

FIGURE 5

"This shows that he was a Dreamer."
—Steven D. Shawley

Horses, disks, and the floral shapes have preliminary contours drawn in black pencil. Incomplete floral shapes at upper left are not sketchy or unsure but are made of three bold, unbroken guidelines. (Those familiar with Plateau beadwork will notice that these floral figures are similar to the kind found in Plateau stylized beadwork motifs.) All completed positive shapes were filled in with either red or black pencil. The word "Sun" is in India ink.

Two disks hovering above the horses have seemingly highlighted areas, making them look shiny and round. Mention of shining disks comes up occasionally in Plateau life and lore. Coyote manages to escape from vengeful characters in the legends of various Plateau people by means of either a disk, the sun, or what is described as a "glittering ball." Followers of Smohalla, the prophet credited with popularizing the Dreamer religion and its similar movement among the Nez Perce, wore "large round silver plates or such other glittering ornaments as they possessed," when dressed for their ceremonies.[16] If the artist did indeed attempt to depict highlights on shiny disks, his perception of light and texture was extraordinary considering a lack of formal training!

At first glance, the black horse appears to have reins, but a close inspection suggests that the single black line is a disregarded guideline for the neck, as is the line visible on the horse's neck below the mane.

What is most noticeable about this drawing is its symmetry, or maybe duality. A red disk floats above the nearer red horse, a gray-black disk above the more distant gray-black horse. The red horse is facing toward red floral shapes. Were the unfinished floral shapes in front of the black horse to be black?

Only guesses about the meaning of this drawing can be made. Deward Walker, Jr., tells us that Christian missionaries emphasized that the universe was divided into good and evil segments "ruled respectively by God and the Devil. . . . This dichotomous view of the universe (so popular among missionaries) was communicated with great vigor by metaphors such as left and right, below and above, dark and light, and black and white."[17] These teachings, or any of the dualities that existed in the artist's day, could have provided inspiration for the picture: day and night, life and death, present and future, white and Indian. But care must be taken to avoid interpreting this or any drawing in the *Cash Book* from the viewpoint of non-Indian culture. A statement made by a Nez Perce elder viewing this drawing may give a more realistic, though less grand, interpretation: "Horses stand this way, real close together, on hot days. Their tails, they swat each other's flies."[18]

FIGURE 6

*"Native American Indians are highly religious,
worshiping their Creator, observing religious rules and
rituals and founding their beliefs and religious traditions
on relationships with Mother Earth, sun, moon and stars.
To Native Americans, nature is all powerful."*
—Mari Watters

All shapes were defined with preliminary outlines drawn in black pencil. Both red and black were used for fill-in work. Cross-hatching with black pencil on the man's shirt and leggings indicates plaid material, a simple yet effective way to get the point across. Again, one wonders if the artist was trying to depict three-dimensional forms when drawing the spiky star in the center of the page, or even the crescent on which the man is standing. The word "Sun" is in red pencil.

Although the page is divided into three separate drawings, they are all related to the artist's ʔipnu cililpt faith. The fact that the page has three drawings may or may not be related to the sacred number *three* in Plateau culture.

Beginning with the images in the center of the page, groups of three elements are obvious. The resemblance of the lower figure to a star or celestial body is likely more than coincidence, celestial motifs playing such an important part in the visual elements of the ʔipnu cililpt faith.[19] Near the upper bar or "level," with the three spikes, flies a bird. Meadowlark (*Sturnella neglecta*) and raven (*Corvus corax*) were known among ʔipnu cililpt believers to deliver messages from the land of spirit and from the natural world to devout humans who would listen.[20]

Another bird makes its appearance, this time atop a pole in the left-hand drawing. This probably represents a wooden likeness of Bullock's oriole (*Icterus bullockii*), whose importance was recognized by the religious leader Smohalla. Smohalla erected a flagpole which he topped with a carving of this sacred bird. The bright-colored Bullock's oriole makes quite a show as it returns to the region in the spring, chattering in the pines as if calling the earth to new life after the winter. These renewing seasonal cycles parallel the hopes of the faithful ʔipnu cililpt followers that the world would soon be reborn in its aboriginal form.[21] Above this little bird hovers a crescent moon emblazoned with three stars. Below the bird, at the base of the pole, is another star symbol and what may be a cluster of feathers.

At far right is a man, a ʔipnu cililpt worshiper as indicated by his aboriginal-styled clothing and his hand and arm position.[22] Much of the material for his clothing is of white manufacture, but the cut and decoration are traditional Native style, a rejection of the outright use of white clothing styles worn by the Christianized reservation Nez Perce. He stands on a crescent moon. Beside him is a pole decorated with feathers, another visual sign of ʔipnu cililpt worship.[23]

Several black pencil line drawings lie unfinished within the bounds of this page. Between the left margin and pole with the little bird atop stands a man with what appears to be a star motif on his wide breechcloth. He may even be grasping the pole. Physically, his proportions in no way equal the accuracy of the man drawn at right. Perhaps this is why the drawing was left unfinished. Two circular disk-like forms are seen in the lower left section, one having the beginnings of a bird or star shape in the center. The purpose of these remains unclear. The faded shapes in the center are caused by the transfer of black outlines from horses on the facing page (figure 7).

All six horses were first outlined in black pencil and then filled in using red and black pencils. Though they prance as usual from right to left across the page, conspicuously missing in this composition are hoofprints, commonly drawn in to imply action. But the active positioning of the horses' legs is all that is necessary to get the point across. The artist demonstrates unusual skill in attempting the muscle structure of the horses, as well as implying perspective, showing the natural clustering of the herd through use of overlapping forms.

The caption "Soldier Horse" does not seem to be one of the unrelated headings. Its orientation to the binding is the same as the drawing's, and it shows no transfer of wet ink to the facing page as do many of the quickly written headings believed to be related to some other business.

Horses were invaluable to the Nez Perce in their attempts to stay a step ahead of the U.S. military. Unlike the pursuing soldiers, who had only themselves and their supply train to look after, the Nez Perce had to move their entire community—women, children, lodges, utensils, and personal possessions. Sadly, injured horses or those so weary they were no longer useful had to be left behind by the fleeing Nez Perce. Warriors took advantage of any opportunity to add to their people's herds. Loose or lightly guarded soldiers' horses were a desirable target for Nez Perce raiders. Besides, it would be impossible for soldiers without mounts to chase or attack a mobile Nez Perce camp. Despite the lack of brand marks on the horses, the halters visible in this drawing imply that these horses belonged to, or were taken from, whites.

Whose horses were they? The Nez Perce acquired soldiers' horses in several ways, including taking them from the battlefield as spoils of war. Because of heavy losses from Perry's and Trimble's soldiers at the White Bird battle, riderless horses, along with a documented sixty-three rifles and accompanying ammunition, may have been acquired.[24] If these are soldiers' horses fresh from combat, though, they ought to be pictured with saddles and other military accouterments attached instead of only halters.

Not wanting to leave civilian horses behind to fall into the hands of the pursuing military, the Nez Perce were reported to have stolen 250 nonmilitary horses in the vicinity of Bannack, Montana, in August 1877.[25] It is unlikely, however, that this drawing represents those stolen civilian horses. The civilian owners usually had them stripped of their tack before placing them out to pasture or in the corrals, which is where most horses were recorded to have been acquired by the raiding Nez Perce. Yet another possibility, and a quite likely one, is that these were horses taken from the "Mount Misery" fight.

Edward McConville and sixteen volunteers were trapped by Nez Perce warriors on top of a hill called Possossona. The whites dismounted and entrenched, making breastworks from available natural materials as well as from their saddles. While the whites hid in their shelter, Nez Perce warriors ran off forty-eight of their horses. The breastworks would account for the lack of saddles on those horses. After spending an anxious, sleepless night in a dry camp, the whites renamed the hill "Mount Misery." Later the Nez Perce found that these were some of the horses that originally belonged to Lookingglass's band. They were taken by soldiers after routing Lookingglass's camp during a July 1, 1877, attack, and were then issued to McConville's volunteers. Upon capturing the horses from McConville's men, the warriors went back to the Nez Perce camp and returned the horses to their rightful owners.[26]

FIGURE 8

"Pretty outfits. These are true warriors."
—Nancy Halfmoon

*". . . They arranged themselves in martial style, the chiefs
leading the van, the braves following in a long line,
painted and decorated, and topped off with fluttering
plumes. In this way they advanced, shouting and singing,
firing off their fusees, and clashing their shields."*
—Irving, *The Adventures of Captain Bonneville*

Initial outlining as well as detailing and texture work
was done with black pencil. Blue and red pencils
were used for the fill-in. These three riders represent
some of the elite of the Nez Perce warriors, as indicated by their outfits. Dressed more for show than
for battle, they are participating in a warriors' parade
around the camp. One such parade occurred at
Tepahlewam, and started the string of events leading
to Nez Perce retribution. Another parade was staged
the second night at the Big Hole encampment.[27]

Most of the Nez Perce went into camp at the Big
Hole River expecting the pace of their flight to slow
down a bit. Many felt that General Howard's troops
had been left behind in Idaho. A time for rest was
badly needed. The second afternoon of the encampment, the warriors dressed in their finest regalia and
paraded around on horseback singing and having a
good time. Of this parade and gaiety, Yellow Wolf
stated, "It was the first since the war started."[28]

In the 1870s, headdresses such as worn by these
men were reserved for war or important ceremonies,
not for casual dances or gatherings. Either parade, at
Tepahlewam or at the Big Hole camp, would qualify
as an important event. Wide red wool trailers, with
feathers attached so they lie flat against the cloth
rather than sticking out as on the well-known Plains

warbonnets, show these to be an older style head-dress, even for the 1870s. Such regalia identifies the men as experienced warriors. The headdresses were most likely acquired or assembled in the warriors' younger days.[29] Feathers tipped with either hackles or horsehair dyed red, such as the ones seen on these bonnets, were commonly associated with war honors. Even in recent times the use of red-decorated feathers has usually been reserved for combat veterans.[30]

The lead rider displays what appears to be a Springfield carbine of the type carried by the cavalry. This may indicate that these warriors had already seen action against U.S. troops, picking up weapons as spoils after the battles. The second rider carries a carbine of a different model, having a barrel-mounted rear sight. Sixty-three rifles including ammunition belts were picked up after the battle at White Bird Canyon. Yellow Wolf tells of acquiring weapons and ammunition from fallen soldiers: "Took guns and cartridge belts from those (dead) soldiers. That is the custom of war. Those guns afterwards were used by other Indians." It should be noted that rifles of this sort are reported to have been in the hands of Nez Perce men prior to the hostilities.[31]

Decorated shields are carried by the leading two riders. The first displays a crescent moon motif. Designs painted on the soft hide shield cover served to increase the shield's protective spiritual power. The actual shield, made of tough bison neck hide or possibly several layers of elk rawhide, would be found underneath the soft decorated cover.[32]

Honor marks are shown painted on the front and rear flanks of the horses, serving a function much like that of modern military ribbons. Colored bars or stripes tell, in typical Plains style, the number of war exploits achieved by the riders. Painted designs on horses may also be intended for spiritual protec-tion or to advertise and enhance the horse's physical power. Especially conspicuous is the handprint on the lead horse. Though painted designs on horses have no universal interpretation, a handprint often symbolized that both horse and rider were responsible for overcoming an enemy.[33]

What looks like a lump on the horses' tails is tail hair that has been gathered and tied. It was the idea of tying the tails that seemed important, not the method of tying; the use of leather thongs, colored cloth strips, or simply tying an overhand knot in the long tail hair itself would meet the objective. The knot kept the horse's tail out of the way and, along with other decorations, was said to help the owner tell his horse from others if he became dismounted in close fighting where kicked-up dust and clouds of black powder smoke drastically reduced visibility. Crow tribal member Thomas Leforge explained further: "This tying up of the horse's tail was to enable it to run faster. I do not know to a certainty whether or not this arrangement effects that result, but the old Indians used to say it did, so it became my practice to do it."[34]

Fancy riding "blankets" were in style in the late 1870s, as shown by this and other drawings in the *Cash Book*. Skins of bear, mountain lion, wolf, bison, and otter, often backed with red wool trade cloth, made handsome alternatives to woven trade blankets.[35] Horse owners may appreciate the training and discipline necessary for a horse to allow a mountain lion skin to be draped over its back as a riding blanket. A somewhat doughnut-shaped pad saddle may have been in use with these blankets, but it is the blankets themselves that attract the attention.

Such a display of artistry and war honors as shown in this drawing enhanced the sense of pride and unity felt within the family and community.

FIGURE 9

". . . we perceived a great body of men issuing from the camp, all armed and painted, and proceeded by three chiefs. The whole array came moving on in solemn and regular order. . . . Soon after the women, decked in their best attire, and painted, arrived, when the dancing and singing commenced."—Alexander Ross

*A*ll the forms were first outlined in black pencil before being filled in with red, blue, and black. Black pencil provides the detail of necklaces and facial features. Most artists have a tendency to focus on the subjects' faces, ignoring the less interesting forehead area. Misplaced eyes high up on the head, as in this case, can be the occasional result. Lack of practice in depicting the female form and dress may have given the artist some trouble with the two foreground figures wearing red dresses. He apparently struggled

with the position of their waists, but true to life, each woman has her individual characteristics not only in height and outfit but in hair texture and facial expression.

If the drawing in figure 8 does represent a parade, little stands in the way of concluding that these women were also participating, maybe as spectators, much as Ross describes above. Like the men in figure 8, they are dressed up. Even their cheeks and the parts in their hair are painted with red paint. The red paint, in fact, is a major indicator of the point of this drawing. These women wanted to look good for their men, and the usual everyday primping wouldn't do. By including face and hair paint, the artist shows us that the women were attending an important community function. Their moccasins, however, remain undecorated, as was the style with

Nez Perce women prior to 1900, and calf-length cloth or hide leggings ensured the required level of modesty for respectable Indian women.[36]

Leather dresses are conspicuously absent. Instead, these women wear brightly colored cloth "wing" dresses decorated with silk ribbon or wool trim. The large, full-cut sleeves resemble the outstretched wings of a bird, thus the name given this kind of dress.[37] Accessories consist of necklaces and beaded belts. The two ladies in front in red dresses are probably wearing necklaces of shell or glass disk beads. Salmon vertebrae have also been strung and used for necklaces and would probably be drawn much like those pictured here. On the right side of the drawing, the lady in blue slightly behind the middle lady seems to have a neck ornament made of dentalium, or "tusk" shells (*Antalis [Dentalium] pretiosum*).

Each dress is gathered by a belt. At far left, the woman wears either a long woven sash or has a decorated leather pendant, occasionally called a "belt tab," hanging from her belt. Oddly, these belts are one of the few instances of the *Cash Book* artist's depicting what is probably beadwork (see figure 31 for an example of beaded moccasins). They are probably the heavy leather belts known as panel belts, with three sections of beadwork embroidery, the intervening sections decorated with rows of dome-topped brass upholstery tacks. Awls were carried in decorated cases looking much like the item suspended from the belt of the red-dressed woman in the center. As the parading warriors proudly displayed the tools of their trade—shields, weapons, and medicine items—a well-dressed woman took as much pride in wearing objects related to her trade, such as a decorated knife sheath or awl case. She really had no intention of sitting down to do some sewing during the celebrations.

The woman in the middle and the one at the far right have what may be scars or decorations on their arms. Mutilation, the cutting of hair, and wearing disheveled clothing were ways by which mourners showed their grief at the loss of a near relative. Aside from the unidentified marks on the arms, no other signs of mourning are evident. Considering their dressy appearance, the women were not currently in mourning. This clue may help place the event pictured here as early in the conflict, prior to heavy Nez Perce losses such as those experienced at the August 9th battle on the Big Hole River. These marks are therefore more likely to represent paint or tattoos. Yet even with this suggestion, little evidence has come to light regarding arm painting, scarification, or tattooing among Nez Perce people.[38]

The contribution of women to successes in the 1877 war cannot be underrated. Care of the camp was their main job. Preparing the food, caring for the children, and setting up and taking down the lodge and its furniture, especially at times of retreat such as at the Clearwater and Big Hole battles, gave necessary support to the defending warriors; and giving the men moral support and encouragement, as well as the reason to fight, helped curtail further losses at the Big Hole.[39] Some women were noted for giving direct aid to the warriors by unbuckling cartridge belts from fallen soldiers and delivering the ammunition to their men.[40] It was at the Big Hole where Walaytic's wife died on the battlefield after obtaining a rifle and killing the soldier who killed her husband.[41] "People tend to think that the men were the heroes of the war," one interviewee commented, "but to me the women that had to gather up the deceased people, they had to take care of the orphan children. To me, these were strong women."[42]

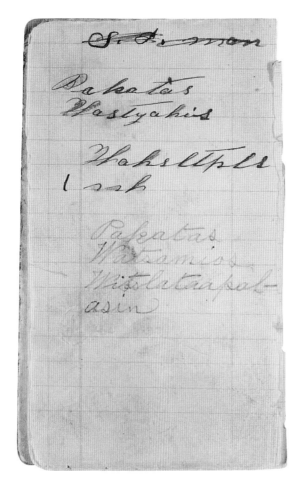

"This post was held by the flower of the Nez Perce warriors. . . ."—Lucullus McWhorter, *Hear Me, My Chiefs!*

The writing on the upper half is in India ink, with the words "Pakatas," "Wastyahis," and "Wahsltpls nh" retraced in red pencil. The formal writing in India ink may have been done during a narration or an interview. The red pencil tracing over the India ink could be idle doodling or perhaps an attempt by the artist to gain practice at cursive writing by going over the words of his scribe. Note that the "S. I. Man" has been scratched out, further indicating that the original purpose of the *Cash Book* was abandoned in favor of its current use. Below the India ink renditions of the three names appears a second version of these names written in black pencil.

The quote above from *Hear Me, My Chiefs!* is taken from a description of the warriors fighting in the Clearwater battle. The three names listed on this page of the *Cash Book* are among those mentioned by McWhorter. Paqatas ʔewyin, whose name is here spelled Pakatas, is also known by his translated name, Five Wounds. In the case of Paqatas ʔewyin, the use of only the first part of his name, Paqatas or Pakatos, is not unusual.[43]

Wacamyos, or Rainbow, was said to have received a portion of his war power from the rainbow, which, like a successful warrior, may be seen but is unaffected by bullets or arrows.[44] The spelling of his name on this page varies from Waslyahis to Watsamios.

Witslahtahpalakin, spelled Witslataapalasin here, is yet another noted warrior. Hair Cut Upwards is the English version of his name. It refers to a Nez Perce men's hair style where the front or bangs are cut shorter than the rest of the hair, are greased or painted, and then are brushed to stand upright. Along with Indian tailored clothing, traditional hair styles helped identify the nontreaty Nez Perce from the reservation Nez Perce. Little else is known of Witslahtahpalakin or his fate.

Paqatas and his "war partner" Wacamyos were well-known bison hunters and experienced warriors. The two missed the initial action of the war while out on the plains hunting bison. Along with a band of hunting companions, they joined the fleeing Nez

Perce camp at Lahmotta the day after the White Bird Canyon battle. Both had gained war experience fighting against the Shoshoneans and the Lakota, and were immediately accepted into the war councils of the camp. The two figured prominently in the destruction of Lieutenant Rains's command at Cottonwood Creek and during the battle on the Clearwater against Howard's troops. A "war mate" relationship between the two young warriors had been pledged at the time of their fathers' deaths, both older men dying together in a fight on the Plains. This pledge involved not only supporting each other in battle but dying together as well, as their fathers had. The pledge was fulfilled at the battle in the Big Hole Basin, Wacamyos dying first in the early morning assault on the camp, and Paqatas falling while charging the soldiers in his grief at the loss of his friend.[45]

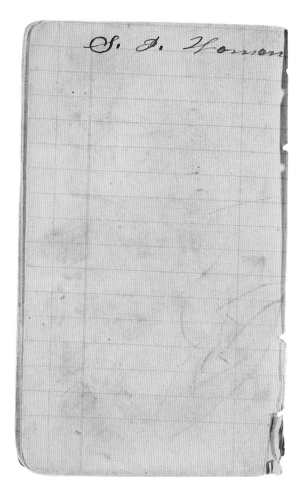

FIGURE 11

The heading "S. I. Woman" is in India ink and was probably intended as a companion to the "S. I. Man" in figure 10. It is curious that both headings were written upside down according to the orientation of the lined pages in the booklet.

Suggestions as to the meaning of the initials "S. I." include Spalding Idaho, Superintendent of Indians, and Sahaptin Indians. Sahaptin is occasionally used as the name for the language of the Nez Perce people, but the Nez Perce people call themselves Nimipu or Nez Perce, not Sahaptin.[46] Further, the term "Nez Perce" instead of "Sahaptin" is written in the *Cash Book* in figures 25 and 43, and again in Agent War-

ner's own hand on the insert. The implication here is that the term "Nez Perce Indians" would more likely have been used in any preparatory headings instead of anything referring to "Sahaptin Indians."

Undefined marks or scribbles in both red and blue pencil appear on this page, as do some fingerprints near the outside margin.

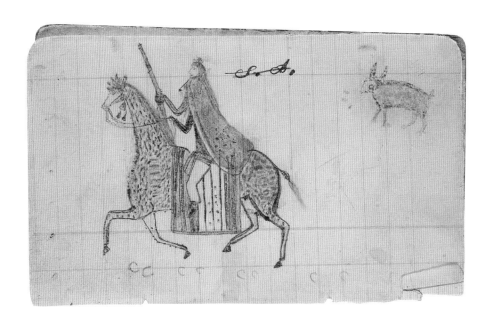

FIGURE 12

"They wore red capes like that, warriors did. They were made of red wool or an elk hide painted, you know, red. They went out of style when all the warriors were killed."
—Nancy Halfmoon

A heading "S. I." in India ink has been deleted with a stroke from the same pen that created it. Horse, rider, and the little creature in the upper right were all outlined in black pencil before the red, blue, and black pencils were used to add color and pattern.

As the men of the Nez Perce tribe assembled for the May 3, 1877, council at Lapwai, supervising General O. O. Howard described their appearance: "The men's faces were painted, the red paint extending back into the partings of their hair—the men's hair braided and tied up with showy strings—ornamented in dress, in hats, in blankets with variegated colors, in leggings of buckskin and beaded and plain moccasins."[47] This drawing shows a man dressed much as Howard described. The warrior wears his fancy clothes and has a pretty blanket on his horse. His forehead, possibly his hair as well, is painted red. Instead of buckskin leggings, his are of blue wool and have a typically Nez Perce style decorative cloth panel around the cuff, though the panel is not as large or as ornate as is seen in photographs of Plateau men in the late 1800s and into the 1900s.

References to red capes such as this man wears are scarce in Nez Perce ethnographic literature, and none of the actual items have yet been identified in museum collections. Drawings in the *Cash Book*, however, show undeniably their relation to warrior dress in the 1870s. The fact that among the Nez Perce these capes are rare in later photographs and in ethnological studies helps bear out Mrs. Halfmoon's poignant statement, above, that capes went "out of style" as Nez Perce culture finally adapted to the reservation lifestyle.

This man seems to be carrying a Winchester, or similar rifle, having an under-the-barrel magazine tube. A clear view of other characteristics such as the frame and finger lever are obstructed by the drawing of his hand, making positive identification difficult.

His horse is decorated, its tail tied up in preparation for a war parade. It has a headdress of decorated feathers, and has ornamental tassels, probably of horsehair, suspended from its neck. The bridle is one of white manufacture, for links of an iron bit and lead chain are evident. The horse itself has been the subject of quite a bit of inquiry. Is this a shaggy or curly haired animal, or possibly a "snowflake," "speckled," or "flea-bitten gray," one with a coat covered with flecks of a contrasting color, or even what is known as a leopard Appaloosa?[48] A close examination of the drawing shows that the dark flecks on the horse not only were meant to show coloration but texturing as well, being drawn so that they stick out beyond the outlines of the horse. Actually, *feeling* any change in texture between differently colored areas on Appaloosas is difficult, but the difference can be *seen*: spots of fluffy, dark-colored hair stick out from the flatter, satiny texture of the light-colored hair. Pretty horses sporting a variety of natural coloration—be they Appaloosas, Dapples, Pieds, or Paints—are reported to have been favorites especially for parades and other public appearances, including warfare.[49] Enhancing or even faking a horse's coloration by adding painted spots wasn't unknown among Native people, but the 3-D effect of the raised spots on this horse's forelegs would be characteristic only of natural coloring. That the Appaloosa was not the legendary, sole, or even common Nez Perce parade or war horse is fairly well documented by the number of non-Appaloosas pictured in the *Cash Book* drawings; however, this horse, and probably one in figure 17, certainly could be Appaloosas.[50]

A little animal is seen in the upper right corner of this drawing with three lines coming from its mouth. Every warrior had one or more special spirit helpers. Though it would have been unusual to display so openly someone's spirit helper, that seems to be what the artist has done in this drawing.[51] The three lines from the little animal's mouth indicate his spiritual power or message. Like one's breath and like smoke from a pipe or incense, a voice also is believed to have the ability to carry spiritual messages.[52]

This is a drawing in what might be called the portrait series. The main purpose of several drawings in the *Cash Book* seems to be to portray individuals rather than an event. It is not difficult to imagine this rider participating in the same parade as those in figure 8.

FIGURE 13

"We saw the big gun on a wagon with men. Four,
maybe six, mules hitched to that gun wagon. . . .
Tenahtahkah dropped the right-hand lead mule.
The cannon was completely stopped."
—Yellow Wolf to Lucullus McWhorter

The writing in India ink retraced in red pencil, and traces of India ink transferred from figure 14 are evident at the outside margin.

Tenahtenkah Weyun, whose name in English is Dropping from a Cliff, was a Nez Perce warrior whose fame in the 1877 war became part of history when Yellow Wolf credited him with participating in the assault on Gibbon's howitzer at the Big Hole battle. He was one of the first to attack the howitzer which rolled up to shell the Nez Perce camp on the Big Hole River. Tenahtenkah killed the lead mule of the team pulling the howitzer, thus effectively stopping its advance toward the village. The name on this page is probably referring to this individual.

FIGURE 14

*"Whips were kept in the possession of mounted Indians
at all times. They might serve as weapons in a fight.
Men also found their whips useful implements
for beating their wives if they misbehaved."*
—John C. Ewers, *The Horse in Blackfoot Indian Culture*

The writing is in India ink and blue pencil, and
"S. I." has been crossed out. Two spellings of LaʔAmninnim Husus's name were attempted on this page;
the first, in India ink, was partly retraced in blue
pencil and then crossed out. The second version,
such as it is, is in blue pencil. Laʔamninnim is the
likely candidate for the honor of *Cash Book* artist,
and this may be his self-portrait (also see figures 40
and 42).

Horse and rider both were first drawn in contours
with black pencil to define the shapes, then color was
added with red, blue, and black pencils. Another
red-caped rider, a possible parade participant, guides
his horse from right to left across the picture plane.
Hoofprints help emphasize the action and direction.

Instead of carrying a firearm, this rider carries a
carved wooden quirt, the lashes of which can be seen
protruding below the horse's neck. These quirts had
a dual purpose: to whip the horses to move faster,
and to serve as clubs. Quirts of this design were
carved of ash or other local hardwood. This style
looks like a series of stacked cones but is actually
one piece of wood, and the finished carving was
none too delicate. A rider wielding one of these
heavy quirts could knock an enemy completely off
his horse and cause serious injury. This method of
fighting would of course require close quarters,
enhancing the reputation of a warrior brave enough
to attempt it. Whips and quirts were recognized as
symbols of authority and achievement. Men and

women both are still honored by being selected "whip person" at dances and ceremonies; their duties include keeping order and ensuring participation by encouraging laggers to get out on the dance floor.

These elaborately ornamented parade horses show the high regard in which horses were held by the Nez Perce. A feather head ornament is tied to the horse's forelock, and horsehair tassels hang from the bridle, which differs from the one pictured in figure 12 by having a small-linked lead chain. Incorrectly called a martingale by some, a red decorative bandolier, or collar, graces the horse's neck. Painted lines on the horse's shoulder probably indicate the number of the rider's successful battles or "coup," a system of war honors learned from the Plains people. Below the shoulder lines, a red dot may represent a different type of honor or may mark the place where the horse was, in the past, wounded, thus further identifying the horse with its rider as a warrior. Such honor marks have basic concepts in common but no truly standardized symbolism, and could not be universally "read."

The striped riding blanket is a trade item, but it should not be mistaken for a Hudson's Bay "candy stripe" blanket, designed in white with multicolored stripes at each end, a style more popular in the Canadian Plains and Blackfeet country. A number of blanket manufacturers' styles and designs were available to the Nez Perce, though aesthetic preferences in this area of the Plateau leaned toward blankets with an all-over design or with a background color other than white.

This horse shows heavy black outlines along the top and on to the croup, or rump, as well as on the chest, hocks, knees, and forearms, which may represent an attempt at depicting form through shading.

La?amninnim is dressed in his finery rather than in clothing he might wear into battle had he time to prepare. His hair, though, is tied up in a special way, probably as he was instructed by his spirit helper in a dream or vision (also see figure 35). Husus ?ewyin, yet another noted Nez Perce warrior, told of a gun battle between him and an infantryman during the Big Hole fight: "My hair in front was all tied up in a bunch, and the shot going through that, the strong bullet just chipped my hair. I still have a strip of wolf's hide with which I tied my hair at the time I was shot in this fight."[53]

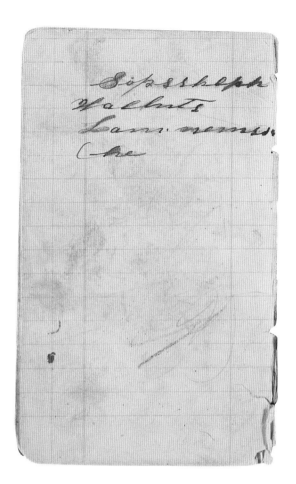

FIGURE 15

"Early morning came news that … Sarpsis Ilppilp
and Wahlitits had been killed."
—Husus ʔewyin to Lucullus McWhorter

*T*he writing is in India ink, retraced with red pencil. The remainder of the page has, for the most part, undefined scribbles in blue and black pencil although near the center there is a triangular shape resembling the front of a tipi, its top oriented toward the binding. Notice the India ink stains transferred from figure 14.

Three young but prominent Nez Perce warriors have their names recorded here. First is Sapsis ʔilpilp, or Red Moccasin Tops. Sapsis was one of the three young warriors who first rode off from the Tepahlewam campground to avenge the wrongs done to his people.

Walaytic, or Shore Crossing, another of the three original avengers, is the second name on this list. It was Walaytic who initiated the Salmon River reprisals. Both Sapsis and Walaytic fought prominently throughout the duration of the ensuing war, and both lost their lives at the battle on the Big Hole River.

The third name is that of LaʔamninnimHusus.

FIGURE 16

The heading "S. I." is written in India ink.

FIGURE 17

"This, the red [paint] on top, is the mark of a warrior. Our young men still do this."—Nancy Halfmoon

Black pencil guidelines delineate all shapes. Red, blue, and black pencils were used to fill in shapes and add detail.

These two riders may be members of a parade, perhaps the same parade as pictured in figures 8, 12, and 14. That these two are pictured together may be significant. Occasionally two warriors make a vow to be "war partners" or "war mates." They fight as a team, covering and aiding each other. Even in times of peace they share camp and family responsibilities as if they were brothers. As with Paqatas ʔewyin and Wacamyos, the vow extends till death; if one of the two is killed in battle, the other is expected, if not encouraged, to charge the enemy or take a similar action which in all likelihood will result in his death as well.[54]

Both men carry carbines, the logical choice of firearm for mounted warriors. The *Cash Book* artist's ability to render detail on such a small picture plane is evident in the clear drawing of the carbine carried by the rider on the right. Both warriors indicate their previous war experience by painting their foreheads with red paint and having their horses decorated with honor marks. Occasionally an individual

will receive special instructions from his spirit helper regarding personal adornment. Barred hawk feathers tied into one warrior's hair, instead of the usual golden eagle feathers, may reflect some of these special instructions.

Golden eagle tail feathers and painted spots decorate the lead rider's cape. It is likely that only the owner of the cape knew the full meaning of these spots, but similar motifs used within the Plateau have been likened to hailstones, stars, or even puffballs.

For a second time a horse is drawn with markings resembling those of an Appaloosa. (Could this be the same warrior as the person pictured in figure 12?) Faded pale blue streaks on the neck and shoulder of this horse represent paint decorations. The artist seemed to misjudge the extent of the cape a bit, as shown by the overlap of the cape and the horse's hip, which appears to have been drawn prior to the cape.

At right, the warrior wears a cloth shirt and is girdled by a cartridge belt. He wears wool thigh-length leggings, and has a plain red wool breechcloth instead of the more common one made from a plaid shawl. The artist determined where this man's knee should bend by first drawing the form of the warrior's leg, then drawing the legging. It is possible that he left the space for the horse blanket blank because he did not remember the design or pattern that appeared on it. His precision in this and other pictures is consistent, and the importance of identifying individuals by their dress and accouterments was vital, since the facial features are all somewhat standardized and many written names were omitted. Rather than have this warrior misidentified due to guesswork on the horse blanket colors, the artist must have chosen to leave it blank. Maybe he hoped to fill in the colors later. It is my belief that this omission is a significant indication of the accuracy of the drawings in this booklet.

FIGURE 18

"I have an open hand, I can talk peace.
I also have a pistol and can fight."
—Calvin Jumping Bull's interpretation of the
gestures made by the figure at center left

Preliminary outlining and shape definition were done using both blue and black pencil. Details and fill-in work were done with red, blue, and black pencils. The drum and exterior of the tipi covers in particular have both blue and red pencil layers to obtain the darker hue, thus extending the limited palette of the three colored pencils used for most of the drawings.

Three tipis together form a council lodge, establishing the basic structure of this drawing. The darker exterior of the lodge covers contrasts with the red interior, creating, whether intentional or not, the effect of a glowing setting as if from a fire, the shadowed covers conveniently framing the scene. A large drum suspended off the ground by thongs looped over forked sticks occupies the center of this council area. Oversized ceremonial pipes emphasize the importance of this particular council, for thoughtful and prayerful smoking was a prerequisite to such business as making war or making peace. Mounted guards, called *akicita* in the Lakota language, are shown riding around the perimeter of the council lodge, further stressing the importance of this meeting. These select warriors functioned somewhat like security guards for most tribal events.[55] The Nez Perce are not known to have developed structured men's warrior or police societies such as the *akicita*. The observant *Cash Book* artist gives us clues about other participants of this council. Hair styles help identify the majority of council members as people from the Great Plains, probably Lakota in this case. Lakota men parted their hair in the middle, a style worn by women in 1870s Nez Perce culture.[56]

Chiefs and leaders of this assembly can be recognized by their prominent foreground position, and by their headdresses and pipes. Leaders to the left of the drum are probably Lakota. Their outfits, especially the headdresses, are typical of Lakota styles of the day. Red stone pipes made of catlinite are in their possession. The chief to the right of the drum appears to be a visitor, a foreigner, a man from "the people who possess black pipes" of steatite, or soapstone—that is, from the west, or Nez Perce country.[57]

Of the audience or spectators, those men on the left have single eagle feathers worn straight up tied to the back of their hair. Others, especially those on the right, seem to be wearing porcupine-hair headdresses called *roaches*. Strips of red wool fabric wrap around their braids. Roaches, once a symbol of achievement in war, became popular with Native dancers because of their ability to move and bounce, accentuating the dancers' motions. During the 1870s, however, none of these hair or head ornaments had gained popularity with the Nez Perce. Dance and ceremonial regalia such as the roaches, and the presence of the large powwow drum instead of smaller ceremonial hand drums, indicate that a dance or celebration is on the agenda for this assembly.[58]

Considering these visual clues and the theme of events related to Nez Perce life that appear throughout the *Cash Book*, it is not difficult to imagine that this picture chronicles a meeting or council involving the refugee Nez Perce and Sitting Bull's self-exiled Lakota in Saskatchewan near Fort Walsh.

Any one of several such meetings or councils may be pictured here. Early in the Bear Paw siege a delegation of Nez Perce elders headed by Half Moon attempted to enlist reinforcements for their tribesmen who were still fighting back at the Bear Paw battlefield. This delegation was the first to contact the Lakota since the 1877 war began (recall that the Nez Perce did not originally intend to flee to Canada).[59] The Lakota, however, had difficulty with the Nez Perce language and could not understand the location of the battle. Some Lakota were reluctant to rile the Canadian authorities by rushing across the border into battle with U.S. troops.[60] A group of Lakota belatedly ventured to the Bear Paw battlefield but arrived too late to take part in the fighting. The battlefield was empty.

Nez Perce refugees straggled into the Lakota camp sporadically, but the second event which would have called for a formal get-together such as is pictured here might have been the arrival of White Bird's people. Back at the Bear Paw camp while the siege continued, Joseph pitied the wounded and hungry among the Nez Perce. Trusting in promises made by the military, he decided to surrender. Though Joseph was recognized as one of the Nez Perce leaders, within the Nez Perce system of governance no one, not even his own people, was obligated to follow him into surrender. White Bird spoke for those who wished to continue the flight to Canada. He and his followers quietly left the camp the night of October 5, long before surrender. After nearly ten days of traveling on foot, White Bird and his refugees were introduced to Sitting Bull and his mounted guards. This meeting took place outside the Lakota camp but, in keeping with Native custom, a formal council in more comfortable surroundings followed.[61]

It is significant that no whites are pictured in attendance at this council. Major James Walsh and his little band of North-West Mounted Police kept close watch over the refugee Lakota. Walsh was even on hand when Sitting Bull's contingent met White Bird's straggling band as they approached the Lakota camp. Though no direct mention of Walsh's attendance at either of the first Lakota–Nez Perce councils has been uncovered, these were events that Walsh and his superiors would not have wanted to miss.

The Lakota and Nez Perce had not been on congenial terms prior to their Canadian alliance. Yet a common enemy and their common status as refugees transcended the old animosities. As the Lakota reportedly exclaimed to the Nez Perce: "We were enemies a long time. We made peace and now we are brothers. Let us go back and fight the soldiers."[62] Still, if the assessment of this drawing's intent is correct, it seems that full trust had not yet been established between these two people. The Lakota chief (Sitting Bull?) holds out one hand, palm up, as a sign of friendship. He holds a pistol in his other hand as if giving his former enemies a choice; he is willing to make amends or to fight. Still wearing his cartridge belt, a Nez Perce leader (at right facing left) grasps his pipe with both hands, leaving his pistol unattended in his belt or holster, ready to seal the truce.[63]

Yellow Wolf tells of a tense moment during this or a similar council when the Lakota, not familiar with the Nez Perce language, had difficulty understanding why Yellow Wolf would not participate in a peacemaking ceremony that involved smoking a pipe to signify ratification of the truce. Fortunately, through sign language it was made clear that Yellow Wolf's hesitation was not due to any lingering hatred of the Lakota but because his personal medicine, or spiritualism, insisted on a smoking taboo.[64]

If this drawing does in fact represent the formal Nez Perce–Lakota peace council, the Lakota appear optimistic. Only one other Lakota seems to be armed: the fellow sitting second to the left of the drum holds an object shaped like a knife. All others, including the seven drummers, seem more ready for a celebration than a fight.

A variety of artistic devices to give the illusion of depth are used in this drawing, especially with members of the audience. Heads meant to be farther in the distance are higher on the picture plane, have less detail, are smaller, and seem partially overlapped by heads appearing nearer the viewer.

FIGURE 19

*T*he recurring "S. I." is in India ink. Lower, undefined words are in blue pencil. Some retracing in red pencil covers the India ink capital S.

[Followed in the *Cash Book* by four blank pages]

FIGURE 20

"I saw a Sun Dance, oh, maybe it was fifty years ago, where both the leaders and dancers held staffs with flags, but they don't do this now-a-days." — Calvin Jumping Bull

The artist used black pencil guidelines with red, blue, and black pencil fill-in, and a straight edge as an aid to draw the dance staffs and the larger red Sun Dance pole. The bison effigy has layers of black and red pencil to show the thicker fur of its cape.

From the Bear Paw battlefield, the *Cash Book* artist

made his escape to Canada. Living with his Lakota hosts for possibly several years, he had plenty of opportunity to view their customs. He chose to record the high point of the Lakota social and religious year, the Sun Dance. For the ceremony pictured here, a tall cottonwood pole, painted red, is placed in the center of the dance arbor. Suspended from the pole are offerings of red cloth. Effigies of a man and a bison are tied near the top of the pole. In this case, both effigies are probably silhouettes cut from rawhide, then decorated. Conspicuously missing from this rendering of Lakota Sun Dance effigies is the usual oversized phallus.[65]

Three dancers are shown. These are persons who have vowed to participate in the Sun Dance ritual in return for spiritual favors such as success in battle or recovery from illness. The pledges, as the dancers are sometimes called, hold staffs, foliage still attached to the top, with additional red cloth offerings tied beneath the foliage.[66] A kilt or blanket is worn around the waist, covering the legs. Notice that their hair is parted in the middle in typical Lakota fashion.

During the self-denial, self-sacrifice part of the Sun Dance, a veteran of the ceremony, one respected for his wisdom, would circle the arena on horseback in full regalia singing war songs to help the dancers "keep a strong heart" during their ordeal. This is likely the job of the warbonneted man to the right.[67] What appears to be a wound on the horse's midsection is the result of a variation in pressure on the red pencil as the artist filled in the color on this pinto.

Possibly, in an attempt to add interest to the composition and to distinguish one dancer from the other more readily, the artist changes the colors of their outfits, alternating reds and blues for their shirts and kilts. Not knowing these Lakota as intimately as his Nez Perce tribesmen, he may have decided to sacrifice accuracy for clarity.

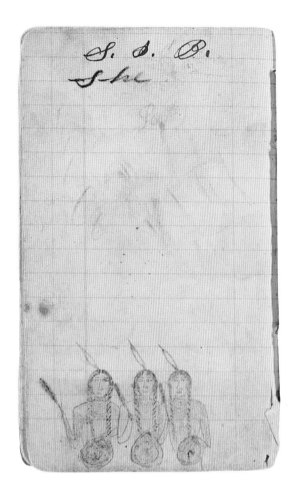

FIGURE 21

"The drum used in the Sun Dance was placed south of the pole. It was a large dance drum of the usual type and elaborately decorated. In addition to the drum a stiff rawhide was beaten."
—Frances Densmore, *Teton Sioux Music*

India ink was used for the "S. I. B." heading, which probably does not relate to the drawing. The blue penciled "She" or "Ske" probably has some relation to the story of the Nez Perce war but has not yet been deciphered. Black pencil guidelines with blue, black, and red pencil fill-in were used for the figures. Black pencil was also used for texturing and patterns.

Between the obvious heading and the depiction of the singers is an expanse of the picture plane containing faded marks in red pencil. Along the left margin are six red arcs whose repetition forms a distinct pattern but which were drawn hastily enough to be easily dismissed as scribbles. Also located on the second line below the blue heading is the beginning of a word, in the same hand as the other writing, but it is as yet unidentified.

Densmore and Blish have explained that Sun Dance music was provided by drummers pounding on a rawhide stretched on the ground. Young Bear and Jumping Bull identified these three Lakota men as Sun Dance drummers, even though they use hand drums made of hide stretched over a wooden hoop instead of a single large drum or a stretched rawhide. Sun Dances involved several days of celebration and ceremony. Variations in the method of providing music for the Sun Dance can change as the dance progresses day by day, or these variations may reflect a regional difference in the ritual.[68]

The hand drums are painted and the drumsticks are made with full, fluffy heads. These singers are dressed in their best outfits, braids are wrapped with red cloth, and they wear what appears to be loop necklaces, an ornament much more common among the Nez Perce than among the Lakota (see figure 24). It is possible that during an earlier friendship ceremony or social gathering an exchange of clothing took place between the two tribes.[69]

The artist may be showing some tribal ethnocentricity in this drawing as well as ones in figures 18 and 20. Aside from the depiction of loop necklaces, this drawing and figure 20 show the principal figures in groups of three, a number with spiritual significance for the Nez Perce people. Figure 18 has the drummers drawn in a group of seven, another number significant in Nez Perce spirituality.[70] Among the Lakota, however, the sacred number would be four or multiples of four, especially for Sun Dance singers.[71]

As in figure 20, the colors of the singers' shirts have been alternated, switching from blue to red, then to blue again.

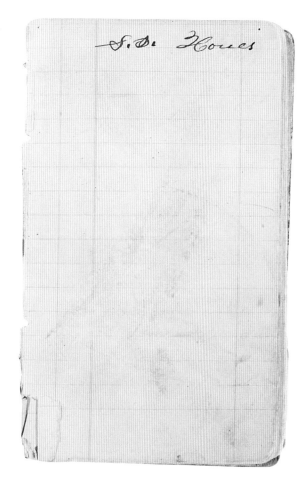

FIGURE 22

"S. I. Horses" is written in India ink. Unidentified blue scribbles occupy the lower center of the leaf.

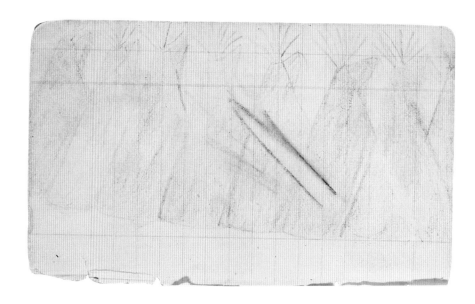

FIGURE 23

"The only time we put up tepees was the place where the buffalo calves used to be found (Big Hole basin)."
—Penahwenomi to Lucullus McWhorter

No preparatory black pencil guidelining is evident in this drawing, with the possible exception of the tipi at the far right. Each tipi is outlined in the color with which it is filled in. Again, alternating colors of red and blue are most likely used to decorate and define individual tipis rather than to portray real painted tipis. The blue scribble is unrelated to the pictorial content of this page.

Determining exactly whose tipis these are, Lakota or Nez Perce, and the location of the camp may not be possible, though evidence leans slightly in favor of Nez Perce ownership or manufacture. The artist assists his audience by giving two, maybe three visual clues. First, the technique of alternating colors from red to blue was used in the two drawings of the Lakota Sun Dance (figures 20 and 21), which suggests that this picture is also related to events in the Lakota camp. Second, the absence of any extension or pendant of material at the base of the smoke flaps fits the cut of Plateau style tipis. And third, red streamers blowing from the tips of the smoke flaps, evident on the three tipis at the right side of the picture, are said to be representative of a tribe other than the Lakota during the late 1870s.[72]

Unless additional information surfaces, it cannot be said for certain that this drawing represents a view of the Nez Perce camp in Canada, but its similarity and proximity to other *Cash Book* Canadian scenes makes this a tempting possibility. The Nez Perce, after the first few months in Canada living among Lakota hostesses (for the women were the true managers of the lodges), formed their own camp, separate from the Lakota lodges.[73]

Other than in Canada, tipis were in use by the Nez Perce during their flight up until the Clearwater engagement. Although the tipi covers were packed, most lodge poles were left at the Clearwater site. As a result, the Nez Perce lived in shelters made of brush and only the tipi covers for nearly twenty-seven nights, from July 12 until probably August 8, when new poles were cut and ready for use the second night of camping in the Big Hole basin. Lodge poles and most tipi covers were abandoned during the retreat from the Big Hole, so the people again resorted to makeshift shelters.[74]

[Followed in the *Cash Book* by two blank pages]

FIGURE 24

"Number 24 is especially remarkable in the portrayal of front-view human figures in carefully detailed clothing."
—John C. Ewers

"Hey, a couple of good-looking guys!"—Dorothy Jackson

Black pencil outlines and detailing, with red, blue, and black pencil fill-in were used for this drawing. A small correction was made in the size of the upper right arm and elbow of the individual at the left, and the original line is still evident, unerased, just outside the finished arm.

This is a portrait of two Nez Perce warriors.[75] Not only does it display a wealth of ethnographic information, but the quality of the composition matches the best of other pictographic work of this time. Its strong vertical symmetry in no way detracts from the unity of the composition. The central tree, rather than splitting the one composition into two, shelters and frames the two subjects with its canopy of foliage. Extensive use of patterns and texturing

throughout the composition unifies all parts of the picture plane. It almost seems as if these two men posed for the drawing, their feet pressing impatiently into the ground as they shifted from foot to foot waiting for the artist to finish. Since the drawing was in all probability produced *after* the incident it depicts, the artist must have had some other motive for including the footprints.

Peeking out from behind the tree in the distance are the heads of the dismounted warriors' horses. Both men have weapons, war clubs with stone heads sewn into rawhide pouches. These loose-headed

clubs delivered a devastating blow, more powerful than the better known fixed-headed clubs of Plains fame.[76] Decorations are suspended from the men's war clubs. The warrior on the left seems to have a striped cloth or scarf tied to the handle of his club. The man on the right has his club handle decorated with an enormous ermine skin. Skins of the ermine or white winter weasel were recognized as the mark of a warrior; as the ermine is fearless in defense of its home and territory, so the warrior defends his family and his rights.[77] This defensive attitude is certainly characteristic of Nez Perce fighting during the 1877 conflict.

A single-compartment bow case and quiver is slung over the right shoulder of the warrior on the right. This is the only depiction of bows, arrows, or quivers in the *Cash Book*. Bows and arrows had a minimal role as weapons in the 1877 war. Of those that were used in combat, most were originally intended only as hunting weapons.[78] Even before the war began, before warriors had an opportunity to acquire weapons as spoils from fallen soldiers, one report states, "The Indians (of the Wallowas) were tolerably well armed with Henry rifles, carbines of various patterns and some few Colts' pistols."[79]

The warrior on the left carries a pistol, the butt visible by his right hip. He also carries a fringed tobacco bag decorated with beadwork embroidery.[80]

Characteristic of the Nez Perce, the men's hair is parted on the side, and the top, or bangs, is cut shorter and brushed to the side. Both wear cloth pullover shirts with a buttoned opening only partway down the front, a style quite common in the later 1800s and into the early twentieth century.[81] Plaid breechcloths and wool panel leggings complete their basic outfits. The red forehead paint is that of a warrior. The man on the left has a cartridge belt around his waist and wears a necklace made from loops of glass or shell disk beads accentuated with a blue bead in the center of each loop, a popular chest ornament for men. Also popular were chokers made of glass trade beads, here shown by a dark blue line drawn around the men's necks just below the chins. Nearly every item of their dress and adornment is of nonnative origin yet has been designed and tailored to fit expectations of a regional style identifying the men as nonreservation Nez Perce.

Variety in the choice of horse gear shows these individuals' personal preferences. The horse on the left is controlled by a commercially made bit and reins; the one on the right has a rawhide or hair rope looped over its lower jaw, serving as a combined bit and reins.

The *Cash Book* artist uses a device in this drawing not often seen in pictographic art. He has drawn a line showing the relationship of the sky to the ground. For some reason he felt it necessary to show the horizon line or at least the hill behind the tree, the warriors, and their horses.

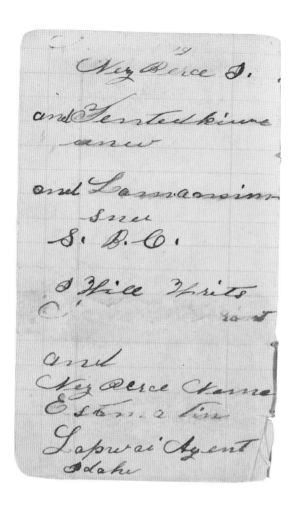

FIGURE 25

"It is . . . likely that there was some other humanely inclined Agency official who smuggled the unfortunates into the Reservation, unknown to the Agent proper."
—McWhorter, *Yellow Wolf*

The page contains India ink writing with some words retraced in red pencil. Adding to other mysteries surrounding this booklet are the obvious erasures on this page and in figure 43.

"Nez Perce I." refers to Nez Perce Indians. "Tentedkiureunw" is almost certainly an attempt at spelling Tenahtenkah Weyun (see figure 13). LaʔamninnimHusus's name appears next in one of its variations. "S. B. C." is as yet undefined. The erasure in the phrase "I Will Write———and Nez Perce Name Estamatin Lapwai Agent Idaho" stands as one of the mysteries surrounding the production of the *Cash Book*. Estamatin, if an individual, is so far unidentified.

The outstanding question here is, why was the name erased? Any Nez Perce refugees returning to the Lapwai reservation were officially to be turned over to military authorities for exile in Indian Territory. Unofficially, the option of renouncing their native religious beliefs to accept Christianity, the agent's authority, and life on the reservation with family and friends was also reported to have been available.[82] The *Cash Book* artist, however, seems to assert his native faith through his drawings in figures 4, 5, and 6, rather than proclaiming a Christian conversion. It is possible, then, that he was allowed to stay at the Lapwai agency by this sympathetic agency employee, at least long enough to produce the *Cash Book* drawings. The "humanely inclined Agency official," if this was the official's pocket notebook in the first place, may not have wanted his name associated with the practice, and so erased it. Comparing remnants of writing left from the incomplete erasure on this page with that left from the erasure in figure 43 indicates the same word, or words, may have been written and erased on both pages.

[Followed in the *Cash Book* by two blank pages]

FIGURE 26

"Later . . . I came to the half bloods on Milk River. They
treated me fine. Boys watched my horse while he grazed.
Knowing I was hungry, they gave me food aplenty.
They gave me new moccasins, for my feet were part naked.
They directed me how to find my people."
—Yellow Wolf to Lucullus McWhorter

Black pencil was used for preliminary outlines,
details, and shadows, and red and blue for most fill-
in, with black used for the center figure's frock coat.
India ink and blue pencil produced the lettering.
Chronologically, figure 26 should precede figure 18.

It is not difficult to imagine this drawing representing the meeting of two self-exiled nations—Sitting
Bull's Lakota representative on the left, a Nez Perce
at far right. In the center, as if making a formal
introduction, is one of the Milk River "half bloods,"
a man of mixed European and Indian ancestry. The
two former enemies, Lakota and Nez Perce, face
each other dressed more for war than for peace; the
Nez Perce wearing warrior's paint and a pistol in his
belt, the Lakota on his split-eared war pony with
rifle and cartridge belt at hand. Between the two is
the Milk River "half blood" without whom the
refugee Nez Perce would have suffered even more
intensely from cold and hunger after their escape
from the Bear Paw battlefield. With no caption for
this drawing, the above scenario must be taken as
speculation—but speculation guided by matching
the drawing's content with historic records. If this,
in fact, is the meeting of Nez Perce and Lakota, the
drawing signals a separation in the Nez Perce story,
the better known part being that of the captive Nez

Perce in Indian Territory, the lesser known story of those who made good their escape and went into exile in Canada.

McWhorter's accounts of the flight from the Bear Paw battlefield tell several times of aid given to straggling refugees by people alternately called "Milk River half bloods," "Crees," or "Chippewa Indians."[83] White Bird and his followers also received aid from these people after escaping from the Bear Paws. The Nez Perce, "coming to a half-breed camp near Milk River," writes Duncan McDonald, " . . . hired one of the party to guide them to Sitting Bull. As they were proceeding toward the Sioux camp, they came upon an Indian skinning a buffalo. The hunter appeared rather shy, but after considerable parley told White Bird that he was a Sioux and that he had come from Sitting Bull's camp."[84] This drawing may then show this Sioux or Lakota buffalo hunter, the half-breed or Metis guide, and White Bird's Nez Perce. On the other hand, it may be showing only the relationships between these three peoples rather than an actual meeting of the three.

Distinct tribal appearances are conveniently shown in this one picture. The hair of the figure on the left is parted in the middle, as was the style among La-kota men; the Nez Perce, far right, has his brushed back or over to the side. A head scarf or bandanna covers the head of the man who appears to be a Metis. His hair is cut shorter than that of the more traditional full bloods on either side of him. All three wear clothing derived from goods manufactured by whites. Differences are shown in the type of trade goods preferred by each group. A plain red breech-cloth provides the requisite body covering for the Plains Lakota. A blanket with a beaded blanket strip is wrapped around the waist of the Nez Perce, recalling the chill of the early October snow in 1877. It would be nice to think that other decorative items, such as this beaded blanket strip, survived the flight to help the refugee Nez Perce keep some appearance of their tribal identity while in exile.

The Metis wears distinctive leggings made either of painted hide or of a common weave of red wool strouding with black stripes. Both the presumed Lakota and the Nez Perce have wool leggings; those of the Lakota man are lacking the characteristic Plateau style panel at the cuff. Both the Lakota and the Nez Perce wear flannel shirts, but the Metis has on a black frock coat. Use of ready-made white trade items was more characteristic of the people with mixed ancestry who lived in both worlds, the Indian and the white, than of the full bloods.[85]

Though characteristic, the Metis outfit is also distinctive. Any of the people of his band should instantly have recognized this individual from the drawing. His striped leggings, head covering, distinctive curvilinear-decorated riding blanket, and his multicolored quirt would reveal his identity.

As in other drawings, the horses have what seems to be shading on their bodies to show their form or roundness.

The languages of the Lakota and the Nez Perce are different enough that virtually no verbal communication initially occurred between these two peoples. The Indian sign language was used and seemed quite effective in most cases.[86] Though the rider on the left appears to be making a sign, it is not detailed enough for precise interpretation. Several native informants were amused by his sign, likening it to a more contemporary obscene gesture.[87]

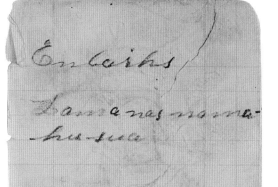

FIGURE 27

The writing is in blue pencil with the first letter of each word roughly retraced in red pencil. The name of La?amninnim Husus appears beneath an unidentified word which, if it follows the pattern set by other words in the *Cash Book*, was probably meant to be an individual's name.

FIGURE 28

"A young man, this [dead] soldier wore a uniform. I took his gun, cartridge belt, and trench-digging knife. I quickly gave the gun and ammunition to a warrior who had none."
—Yellow Wolf to Lucullus McWhorter

All guidelines, including the shadows on the horses, are in black pencil. Red and blue fill in some of the positive shapes. The warrior at the right has a shirt colored by layering black over red pencil. Hints of India ink from a title on the facing page can be seen on the left margin.

Desiring to show spatial relationships between the two horses, the *Cash Book* artist gave some interesting forethought to composition. A blue rear hoof from the lead horse, probably drawn and colored after the trailing horse was drawn, shows just under the shoulder of the trailing horse. No trace of overlapping guidelines from the lead horse which would

give the picture a transparent effect exist. Lines in black pencil define the front shoulder muscle structure of the trailing horse, and give texture to this horse's mane. Ill-defined red scribbles occur over and under the rear of the trailing horse.

Both warriors are Nez Perce. Their brushed-up-in-front hair style and panel leggings make for easy tribal identification. The leggings, especially apparent on the trailing warrior, are in the form of a tube going up the leg only as far as the thigh. A red tie-thong extends from the upper opening of the legging to a belt, acting somewhat like short suspenders. Extra material from the tie-thong, probably a strip of the same red wool used for the legging, dangles behind. The trailing rider wears or may be carrying a coat made from a blue blanket.

Abrasion has worn the color and detail from the lead rider, but the action is clear. He is receiving a gun from his companion, his hand extended to grasp the weapon while on the run. The trailing warrior's hand blocks the view of the hammer and lock mechanism, making specific identification of the weapon impossible, though it is a carbine with a rear barrel-mounted sight and a low-profile trigger guard. Nearly all men had at least one spirit helper but not all spirits enabled men to excel in warfare. Loss of a weapon, as well as suffering a wound or loss of a horse, was frequently the result of weak or absent spirit power associated with war. Often it was the better warriors who, during the confusion of battle, relied upon their experience and spirit power for survival and gave their weapons to less fortunate men—men without adequate war medicine. Stories of sharing and trading firearms are common in oral recounts of the 1877 war, but the incident pictured here probably had a special significance for the artist, such as recounting one of his exploits. Considering the similarity of clothing worn by this warrior to that worn by the men in figures 14, 40, and 42, this may be another view of La?amninnim Husus.

Plainly visible on the rear horse's front right shoulder is a carefully drawn brand. Contacts with brand registries in four states and several counties produced no source for this mark. It is possible that the horse was acquired through trade or raiding, which could put the source of the brand quite a distance away from the Northwest. The writings of Lawrence Kip and Francis Haines (whose account may have been influenced by Kip's report) indicate that the Nez Perce did some of their own branding.[88] To the artist, however, the prominent brand seemed absolutely necessary to identify the warrior riding this horse, and possibly to communicate the intent of this drawing.

FIGURE 29

"I do not care to return home! I want to go with my brothers and sisters. If I am killed, it will be all right."
—Hinmit Tootsikon to his father, Red Heart

The now familiar "S. I." heading in India ink is seen at both top and bottom of this page. Two Nez Perce names are written twice each, once in blue pencil and once in red. The first letter of each blue version is roughly retraced in red.

La?amninnim Husus's name appears twice; the lower, red version has some modifications, including an umlaut above the "u" in an attempt to achieve phonetic accuracy.

The other name is that of Hinmit Tootsikon, or Speaking Thunder, a warrior from Red Heart's band. Several nonwarring but wandering groups of Nez Perce met up with those fleeing from Howard's soldiers. One of these bands was led by Red Heart. When informed of the war, most of Red Heart's people decided to try their luck with agent Monteith back at Lapwai rather than joining their fighting kinsmen. Several individuals, however, chose to fight beside friends and relatives fleeing with Joseph, White Bird, Toohoolhoolzote, and Lookingglass.

Warned by his father that only death awaited him if he fought along with the warring Nez Perce, Hinmit still chose to join the fleeing bands. Hinmit fought bravely through the battles only to die of disease after his surrender and internment in Indian Territory.[89]

[Followed in the *Cash Book* by a blank page]

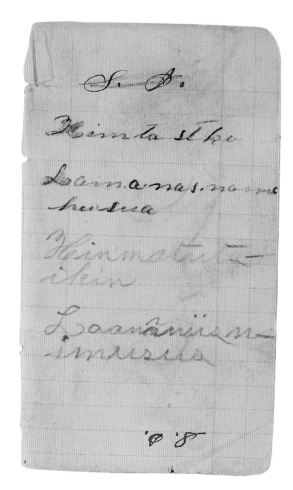

FIGURE 30

*"Wahlitits, Sarpsis Ilppilp, and Tipyahlahnah Kapskaps
were the first to start in the charge, all of the three wearing
full-length red blanket coats of same make and pattern.
These coats were to show their contempt, their fun-making
of the soldiers, to draw their rifle shots,
of which they were not afraid."*
—Weyahwahtsitskan to Lucullus McWhorter

The writing is in India ink, retraced or colored with red pencil. As on other India ink letters, the red pencil seems not so much to have been retraced as simply colored on, much as one would absentmindedly doodle.

Like most other drawings in the *Cash Book*, this one was originally outlined with black pencil. Black pencil was also used for the detail work and for coloring the horse. Red and blue pencils were used to add color to the positive shapes, and to alter the plain black pencil used for the horse.

The word "Pevylune" does not match any names uncovered so far in the literature and records. Nez Perce sources have tried to make familiar sounding words from this, but to no avail. The individual pictured here is undoubtedly one of the "Three Red Coats." Two of the three, Sapsis Ɂilpilp and Walaytic, were involved in the initial Salmon River raids. A war mate, Tipiyelehne Qepsqeps, was the third. These three had the women of the camp sew them bright red, hooded blanket coats called "capotes" (from the French term *capote*, pronounced ka-poᵗ, simply meaning "hooded coat"). Besides their primary function as coats, the capotes served several other purposes. First, they identified the three warriors as those who began the fighting. Lest anyone call these men mere troublemakers who began the hostilities and then shied away from the consequences, their red coats made them conspicuous and showed them always on the front lines of the battles, defending the camp. Second, the conspicuous red coats enhanced their status as warriors by making them easy targets, thus showing off their bravado. Third, the matching coats identified them as a fighting team, three companions who supported each other and added to the powerful and determined defense which drove troops under both Howard's and Gibbon's command a total of six times into retreat or entrenched positions.

Clues other than the undeciphered word "Pevylune," or "Devylune," give an indication as to which of the Red Coats is pictured here. Sapsis is identified in Piyopyo Talikt's drawings as well as in the *Cash Book* (figure 31) by his wolf fur medicine hat and by another wolf hide medicine piece tied to the shoulder of his capote.[90] Sapsis is also reported to have worn a red shirt and a loop necklace, the top strand of which was shattered by the bullet that claimed his life at the Big Hole.[91] Since the red shirt, loop necklace, and wolf hide medicine pieces are missing in this portrait, it is doubtful that the *Cash Book* artist was attempting to depict Sapsis in this scene.

Of the two remaining Red Coats, Walaytic is said to have carried a Springfield carbine.[92] The subject of this drawing, however, holds a rifle of a different model, apparently with a center-mounted hammer but no lock plate. Features from the drawing of this weapon are reminiscent of the configuration of a Remington rolling block or a Maynard breechloader, with the exception of the wooden forestock.[93] Further, Walaytic, like Sapsis, was killed at the Big Hole by a shot to his upper body while he was firing at Gibbon's troops from a prone position behind a log.[94] Close inspection of this drawing shows not an upper body wound but what could be a lower body wound. Tipiyelehne, the third Red Coat, received such a wound while trying to retrieve the body of his cousin Sapsis from the Big Hole battlefield. Piyopyo reported that the wound was "above the hip."[95]

Yellow Wolf describes Tipiyelehne as being "shot through the right side just below the short rib."[96] The wound which seems to be pictured here matches these last two descriptions more closely than the descriptions of either Sapsis's or Walaytic's wounds.

Tipiyelehne survived the Big Hole battle and eventually made his escape from the Bear Paw battlefield. He was murdered before reaching the camp of the Lakotas. Seeking shelter from severe weather he arrived at a camp of Assiniboines who, supposedly under orders from U.S. troops, killed him and other Nez Perce who found their way into their camp. Following Native traditions of hospitality, the refugees were fed and sheltered while inside the bounds of the Assiniboine camp, but once on their way again, were ambushed and killed.[97]

Other features of this drawing include a cartridge belt slung over the subject's left shoulder. The faint red lines on this man's forehead could be traces of paint left from the previous day's fighting or may simply be fading from the original drawing due to age and abrasion.

Tipiyelehne (for that is who this drawing almost certainly represents) holds his favorite war-horse. The horse's ear tips are split, some say for the purpose of making a favored war-hose easy to identify when pastured with the rest of the herd.[98] A symbolic meaning, such as equating the horse's abilities with the speed and power of forked lightning, may be represented by the split ears as well. Dashed lines imply that some sort of action has taken place. Maybe they represent this warrior's footprints, how he dismounted from his horse and walked about. Considering how hot the fighting was at the Big Hole and Bear Paw camps, these dashes could instead represent spent cartridge cases.

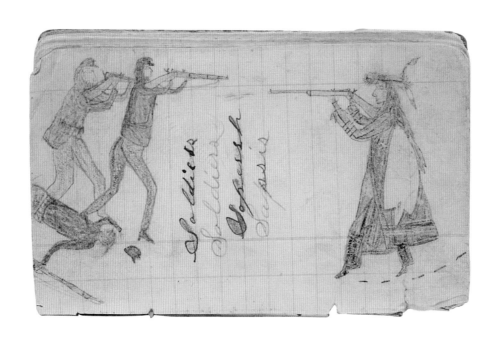

FIGURE 31

"Sarpsis Ilppilp made directly fronting the soldiers,
and killed. I saw him shoot, dropping a soldier."
—Piyopyo Talikt to Lucullus McWhorter

The drawing has black pencil outlines and details with fill-in in red, blue, and black pencil. The writing is in India ink and black pencil, with red pencil applied over the India ink letters.

The scene shows Sapsis ʔilpilp fighting three soldiers at the Big Hole battle. This is another of the drawings where the written names positively match up with the characters. Piyopyo Talikt pictographically recorded this event in a similar way, showing Sapsis wearing his wolf hide hat, or crown, standing away from his tethered horse, having cornered or killed several soldiers.[99] Sapsis has turned his carbine, one almost certainly obtained from the battlefield of an earlier engagement, upon the soldiers. He has killed one, and has just struck the foremost soldier with a second bullet. The puff of smoke from Sapsis's carbine appears simultaneously with that from the infantryman's rifle, but it is Sapsis's bullet, represented by a red dot, which is striking the soldier's chest.

Sapsis wears his red blanket capote and has a wolf hide attached to its left shoulder. Wolf hides, displayed on a capote such as this one, worn as bandoliers, or simply held in the hand, were emblems representing the gift of certain spiritual powers. "Wolf power was highly desired among the Nez Perce Indians for warrior skill, courage, and hunting prowess."[100] Sapsis's long breechcloth is made of a striped shawl. The blue and red moccasins he wears

may be another attempt to show applied decoration such as beadwork (also see figures 9, 24, and 26).

Long rifles help identify the soldiers as infantrymen. The forestock comes nearly to the end of the barrel—the barrel being secured to it by two metal bands rather than one, as is evident at the end of the shorter stock on Sapsis's carbine. Jackets worn by these men are longer than those of the horse soldiers or cavalry, and are typical of uniforms issued to soldiers in the infantry.[101]

The infantry of the 1870s was rather the tail of the dog so to speak, considered by many as having a lower status than the cavalry. The *Cash Book* artist shows the infantry wearing forage caps, a style of hat that by 1877 was determined generally unsuitable by the army as a whole but apparently was still good enough for their infantrymen.[102] In addition, these soldiers are dressed in full regulation uniforms (see also figure 37). Cavalrymen, on the other hand, were allowed to take more liberty with the word *uniform*, tending "to lean towards the flamboyant and individualistic as compared to the infantry."[103] A variety of hats and blouses are shown on the cavalrymen pictured in figure 34. Despite the infantry's lower status, Gibbon's soldiers fought their part of the campaign as well as any other branch of the army.

[Followed in the *Cash Book* by a blank page]

FIGURE 32

"[This] was maybe a charge or a rush to battle for defense.
They didn't have time to dress or paint their horses
[as in figure 8]."—Lynn Pankonin

Outlines, detail, and fill-in were done in black pencil, and red pencil was used for other fill-in work. At first glance this drawing seems to be another parade scene. Compared to the one in figure 8, not only is the direction of action reversed and the amount of regalia reduced, but the mood of the artist seems to have changed, so much that some have suggested that a second artist produced this drawing. Close inspection, however, reveals the same preparatory outlining techniques and delineation of facial features and horse forms as in the previous drawings. These warriors are missing much of the fine regalia associated with parade scenes, yet they are armed as if for battle. Maybe they are mounted for defense, riding from camp to repel an attack such as that on the Clearwater where time would have allowed at least minimal war preparations. Despite sporting horse gear and decorations such as head feathers, collars, and tied-up tails, the horses are missing the usually conspicuous, and time consuming, painted decorations. Any amount of horse decoration would probably not have been evident at either the Big Hole or the Bear Paws battles, where the horses, including

those reserved for war, were pastured away from camp when the surprise attacks were made.

The *Cash Book* artist shows us a variety of weapons, mostly carbines. At far left is a rider who carries a weapon resembling a model 1871 Sharps. Lean Elk, who temporarily took over leadership of the fleeing Nez Perce after the Big Hole battle, was said to have carried a Sharps rifle.

The men are riding on horse blankets made of animal skins. Most have painted faces and extra ammunition in their cartridge belts. A single head feather worn straight up was not a common ornament for Nez Perce men in the 1870s. Mention of head feathers is scant in the literature as well.[104] One warbonnet with feathers lying flat against the cloth trailer can be seen on the lead rider, who also carries a lance or coup stick, used for striking an enemy. What appears to be a crook in the end of this stick, rather like a shepherd's staff, is a style not unknown among the Nez Perce but more typical of Plains people.[105] Could this be a Canadian scene after some trading, gift giving, or acculturation in the Lakota way of life took place?

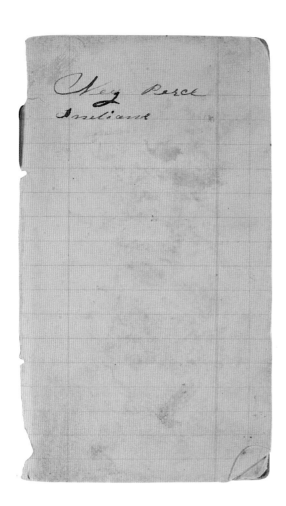

FIGURE 33

"Nez Perce Indians" is written in India ink. This heading may refer to the warriors in figure 32.

[Followed in the *Cash Book* by a blank page]

FIGURE 34

"They're riding in formation, they're not charging. So!
This is an ambush."—Kevin Peters

"Oh, they're [the soldiers] going into a trap!"
—Nancy Halfmoon

"Soldier" is written in India ink. The drawing is one
of the few with figures not outlined in black pencil
prior to coloring. Most shapes have, however, been
outlined in their own color—blue horses and soldiers outlined in blue, red horses in red.

Uncertainty exists as to the event pictured here, but
it is a scene showing cavalry troops riding in formation observed by Nez Perce warriors partly concealed
behind a hill. It is unclear if "Soldier" was written
to explain the drawing or for some other purpose.

This may represent the pending attack on Perry's
command as it approached White Bird Canyon.[106]
The only other incidents that might call for similar
landscape features and characters were the scouting
and defensive maneuvers of the Nez Perce as they
monitored troops under Howard's command prior
to the Clearwater battle.[107]

This drawing emphasizes the mixture of uniform
and nonregulation dress the cavalry was known to
wear while on campaign. Though he certainly had a
blue pencil at hand for drawing standard issue uniforms, the *Cash Book* artist varied the colors of the
cavalrymen's clothing to show the variety of outfits
and hats worn while in the field.[108]

FIGURE 35

"Our choice of a battlefield was mere accident, for we had no water, nor any protection except one or two small trees, and bare, broken, rocky upland, so rocky even entrenching was difficult."—Colonel H. L. Bailey describing the Clearwater battlefield

Most of the outlines are in blue pencil, but red and black outlines exist as well. The words "Soldier" and "S. I." are in India ink, and three Nez Perce names are in blue pencil with some retracing done in red.

Three armed warriors close in on a group of dismounted soldiers. The soldiers have sought shelter at the top of a knoll or hill. Two of the six soldiers are now hors de combat, shot in the head as indicated by upraised arms and a red dot on their faces. The three warriors are wearing the Nez Perce adaptation of white men's goods: cloth shirts, breechcloths made of shawls, and wool leggings with panels or

decorative strips at the cuff. One warrior has his hair tied up much like the man's hair style in figure 14. What may be primary flight feathers from a trumpeter swan (*Olor buccinator*), a bird noted for its spiritual connection with the heavens due to its high flying ability, are tied into this warrior's hair.

All three warriors have cartridge belts, which no doubt previously belonged to their adversaries. Anson Mills is usually credited with promoting the use of cartridge belts in place of stiff leather cartridge boxes hung on soldiers' belts. Many soldiers were known to have made their own cartridge belts, or had them made by a post sutler until 1876 when the military began to issue cartridge belts to servicemen. The military belts were leather with canvas cartridge loops which, unlike belts with leather loops acquired unofficially by the soldiers, would discourage the brass cartridges from corroding and fouling both the belts and chambers of guns. Belts pictured in the *Cash Book* drawings probably represent both types.[109]

Various firearms are evident among these Indians. The warrior with the swan feathers carries what resembles an old model 1865 Spencer carbine.

The artist offers a variety of clues helpful in determining the engagement pictured here, leaving little doubt that the event is from the Clearwater battle. Hardee-style hats and blue uniforms show the soldiers to be dismounted cavalrymen, thus correlating with Yellow Wolf's statement: "This fight [the Clearwater battle] was with cavalry only. Later, foot soldiers came."[110] Red footprints show the Nez Perce defenders' trail as coming from a common place, probably their camp, and they fight from low positions due to lack of natural cover. A series of red semicircles across the top right may represent hills, or a warrior's ducking and diving motions as he fires and then advances upon the soldiers. Bullet-pocked rocks are scattered across the lower battlefield. "The little boulder is good for hiding behind," explained Yellow Wolf, who went on to tell how his uncle fought at the Clearwater "crawling slowly, rolling a boulder ahead" as his only cover. Lack of adequate cover for either offensive or defensive maneuvers characterized the Clearwater terrain.

Although Many Wounds, a survivor of the Nez Perce war, tells of three Nez Perce sharpshooters holding off Howard's troops near the outset of the Clearwater battle, the warriors pictured on this page were probably not the same three.[111] Paqaʔalway-nakt, Joseph, and Kapkap Hayna, whose names appear on this page, are in all probability the three warriors who are pictured here attacking the soldiers. Kapkap Hayna is an individual not yet identified. Joseph, on the other hand, is a name well known to anyone familiar with western history. But popular history usually overlooks the occurrence of two Josephs. Duncan McDonald, giving his version of the Nez Perce side of the war, reminded his readers that there were "two brothers, each named Joseph": Joseph Senior (Chief Joseph) and his younger brother, Joseph Junior, also known as Ollicut. "Indeed, Joseph appears to have been the name of a dynasty rather than an individual," wrote Howard in his memoirs of the war, stating that Chief Joseph's younger brother Ollicut "was frequently called 'Young Joseph.'"[112] Though Ollicut took part in most of the combat situations throughout the war, the Clearwater battle is one of the few in which the well-known Chief Joseph grabbed a weapon and took to the field. If this drawing does picture Chief Joseph in combat, it is a rare glimpse of the combative side of the prominent camp leader.

Questions about the authorship of the text in the *Cash Book* arise again at this point. Was the writer a Nez Perce, recording "Josphe Young" with spelling and syntax influenced by his own language, or was the writer someone else recording Joseph's name verbatim hurriedly from a Nez Perce narrator?

FIGURE 36

"I noticed that the . . . warbonneted Cheyenne who
headed the soldiers in their first attack came riding towards
us. He made the sign to me, 'You see the sun? That sun and
this hour you are going to die.' I threw the sign back to him,
'You shall die first. . . .' Then I stood to meet him.
I shot first, then he shot."—Piyopyo Talikt

Black and blue pencil guidelines delineate the shapes, with red and blue pencil used for fill-in. Red pencil has been applied so thickly on parts of this drawing that it seems almost a different medium, much like red-orange wax crayon. Close inspection of earlier drawings shows the same effect but not as pronounced. "N. Indians" is written in India ink.

Here is one instance of the *Cash Book* artist focusing on an event and a hero that are truly part of the Indian side of the story. White historians either have not realized its significance in Nez Perce history or have been unaware of it. The artist shows Piyopyo

Talikt having a fight with a warbonneted Indian, one of Nelson Miles's scouts. Like the *Cash Book* artist, Piyopyo produced a series of drawings, one showing this same event.[113] His drawing and narrative differ a bit from the version presented in the *Cash Book*. His own drawing shows him dismounted, aiming a rifle instead of a pistol at the Indian. The *Cash Book* artist may not have witnessed this event, drawing his picture based on stories recounting this brave standoff that he heard while in the Canadian camp of the Lakotas. This would account for the variance in weapons and poses between the two drawings.

When Miles attacked the Bear Paw encampment, he assigned Captain George Tyler to capture the Nez Perce horse herd grazing a short distance to the northwest of the camp. Miles's Lakota and Cheyenne scouts charged after the herd also, hoping to claim some of the horses. Piyopyo and several of his people were with the horses that morning, preparing to drive them into camp to be packed for the final leg of the flight to Canada. These Nez Perce were cut off from the main camp. Piyopyo continues his narrative: "I was afoot leading my horse tied to my belt, Indian rope bridle looped about his under jaw. He was jerking trying to get away and my aim was bad. The Sioux rode again making a charge at me . . . but as the enemy made a charge passing me he turned to shoot and I dropped him. . . . I wanted the Sioux's gun and warbonnet but the other Sioux and soldiers, heading for me, I untangled my horse's foot, leapt on his back and galloped way. Looking back I saw the Sioux sitting up removing his warbonnet. I do not know if I killed him or not."[114]

After successfully eliminating the threat from this Cheyenne, Piyopyo was able to return to the Nez Perce camp. There he helped defend the camp from Miles's soldiers until the headmen decided that those who wanted to surrender, instead of continuing on to Sitting Bull's Lakota camp, would give themselves up to the soldiers. Piyopyo slipped out of the besieged camp and headed for Canada only hours before White Bird's people also made good their nighttime escape.

The weather was unseasonably cold for October, and snow had fallen the previous night. For warmth Piyopyo wore his blue blanket capote, which helps identify him in this drawing as well as in his own drawing of the event. He wears a cartridge belt and carries a Colt revolver, which he tries to shoot at his foe from a galloping horse. His wolf hide warrior's medicine piece, probably tied to the shoulder or back of his coat, is noticeable below his capote.

FIGURE 37

"He was just in front of his own tepee. Soldiers were on this side, not far from him. He stood there shooting arrows at the enemies. The soldiers saw, and fired at him. That Indian stepped about a little, but continued sending his arrows. Three times those soldiers fired and missed him. The fourth round killed him."—Yellow Wolf speaking of the warrior Paqa Pantahank

The drawing uses pencil guidelines with black, red, and blue pencil fill-in. The fighting was fierce at the Big Hole River camp. Colonel John Gibbon with his infantry attacked the camp on the morning of August 9, 1877. Soldiers and warriors fought right among the lodges, sometimes firing so close that muzzle blasts left powder burns as well as bullet holes in the victims. "Bullets were singing through the tepee, splintering the poles They came thick, like the summer hail," recalled Two Moons.[115] Paqa, whose last stand was made fighting with his bow and arrows as described above,[116] is not the warrior

pictured here, but the action shown matches Yellow Wolf's description (above) closely. Any number of warriors could have been in this same situation, attempting to defend their homes and families against the infantrymen's invasion. Yellow Wolf tells of two other warriors, Wetyetmes Likilinen and Tiwet Toitoi, who fought in front of their tipis protecting their families.[117]

Dashes drawn around the base of the tipi show spent cartridges or frantic footprints, indicating the desperate fighting that took place. Many of the people were still in their lodges asleep when the attack commenced. The surprise attack gave this warrior with his Winchester rifle no chance to dress or prepare properly for battle. He wears no red forehead paint, and the tails of his long breechcloth are still tucked up into his belt, as was a custom for comfortable sleeping. Yet he and his partially pictured companion direct deadly fire at the long-coated infantrymen.

FIGURE 38

"I rode up on the high flats across the river from our camp. We met with big surprise! Soldiers were passing in a long string of two miles or more. Itsyiyi Pawettes whirled his horse and hurried back down to camp with message that a thousand soldiers were right on us."—Piyopyo Talikt telling of the attack on the Clearwater camp

The original writing on this page was the India ink notation "S. I. Soldier," which appears upside down when viewing the Nez Perce names. Blue pencil spells the names of two Nez Perce warriors. "Soldiers," written a second time in blue pencil, accompanies the warriors' names.

Ɂiceyeye Pewwetes is the first name listed here. He is credited by Piyopyo with being the first to notify the Nez Perce village of the advance of Howard's troops on their camp on the Clearwater.[118] LaɁamninnim Husus is listed next. Occupying space at center page are repeats of the first two names, showing alternate spellings.

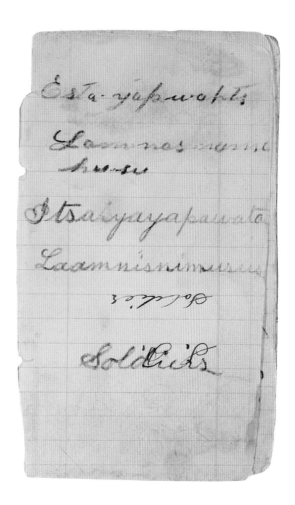

"Twenty minutes into the battle, soldiers had gained control of the southern end of the village. . . . Those who escaped made their way toward the camp's northern end. One was Seeskoomkee, the limbless ex-slave who had warned of the soldier's approach at the White Bird battle, observed alternately rolling and hobbling on his one hand and knees until he gained a shallow depression at the edge of camp."—Hampton, *Children of Grace*

The artist used black pencil guidelines with red, and black-over-red fill-in. Blue colored pencil was used for the letters.

Only one of the names on this page has been interpreted. "Dawatshi" remains unknown, but the other two are both attempts at capturing the sounds of the same name, that of Itskimzekin. Itskimzekin's original home may have been as far south as the Mount Shasta area of California. Plateau trading and raiding parties ventured far from home territory. He was acquired by trade or force, much the way other goods might have been appropriated during one of those excursions, and was kept in a position of servitude, as a slave. Itskimzekin's shorter hair style might be attributed to his years as a slave, for short hair visibly marked a slave's status within some societies.[119]

Itskimzekin was known by a confusing variety of names, including the blatantly descriptive "Seeskoomskee," which means "ends cut off" or "no hands and feet." Accused and convicted of petty theft by one of his owners, he was sentenced to temporary confinement in iron shackles or possibly traps. It was Itskimzekin's bad luck to be forced to serve his sentence during a subzero night, resulting in his punishment far exceeding what was originally intended. The combination of iron shackles and freezing weather contributed to serious enough frostbite that both feet and his right hand had to be amputated. "It cured him of theft," claimed one informant.[120]

Soldiers gained access to Nez Perce camps three times throughout the conflict: first during the attack on Lookingglass's village, second at the Big Hole, and finally momentarily at the Bear Paws.[121] Since records indicate that no tipis were erected at the Bear Paw encampment and considering that Itskimzekin was not associated with Lookingglass's band, this combat scene undoubtedly represents an event at the Big Hole battle. Itskimzekin's kneeling pose and left-handed grip on his revolver reveal his physical disability. He has moved away from the tipis, red dashes representing not necessarily footprints in Itskimzekin's case, but the direction of his movements. Bullets from the enemy, drawn as dashed black lines, whiz past. Oddly, he looks out of the picture at the viewer instead of toward his targets.

Itskimzekin is credited with first alerting the Nez Perce camp at White Bird Canyon of the approaching troops. Though he was said to be suffering the effects of a drinking spree the previous night, his reputation as a good horseman may have been reason enough to recruit him to ride from a lookout position into the sleeping camp shouting the alarm of approaching soldiers.[122] His freedom had since been granted through a system of working off his purchase price by service to his Yakama owner, but Itskimzekin chose to stay in the Plateau area, allying himself to and fighting with Nez Perce comrades, eventually making good his escape to Canada. Itskimzekin chose to live the remainder of his life with the Lakota. His skill as a horseman, especially in breaking wild horses, made him an asset in whatever village he decided to stay.

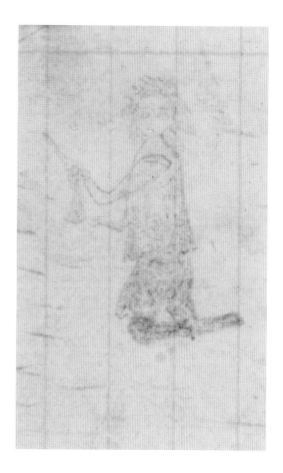

FIGURE 40

*"A Cavalry trooper [is] down and apparently killed
or being killed in the conflict. The hat design is the
'Hardee' style, outlined in blue, [and] the pants
are the typical sky blue color."*—Terry Leaf

Referring to the downed soldier:
"Ooh, I think he's got that one!"—Nancy Halfmoon

Considerable remnants of the red-orange pencil are
left on this drawing. Outlining was done in blue
pencil. A brownish color was achieved by layering in
blue and red-orange. Lettering is in India ink, and
blue pencil.

A variation of La?amninnim Husus's name appears
for the ninth time in the *Cash Book*. Assuming the
names written on the pages refer to the individuals
pictured, this may then be a second view of La?am-
ninnim Husus, brandishing a pistol and wearing a
blue capote. (The red-shirted warrior, if this is the

case, would be ?iceyeye Pewwetes, as explained in
the text for figure 41.) La?amninnim's red wool
blanket leggings clearly show the decorative panel at
the bottom, as well as a dark stripe woven into the
blanketing material. Missing, though, is his distinctive hair style as pictured in figure 14.

The action is fast in this picture. Red bullets fly
from the right side. A soldier, wearing the modified
uniform of a cavalryman rather than the regulation
dress of a long-coated infantryman, has lost his gun,
been shot through the back, dragged off or fallen
from his horse, and is now about to receive the *coup
de hachette* from the red-shirted warrior with the
pipe tomahawk. Large-bladed English type pipe
tomahawks were generally used as ceremonial items
in the later 1800s, but as shown in this drawing they
could be effective weapons in the bloody business of
hand-to-hand combat.[123] Blue dashed lines, representing the soldier's footprints, show how he tried
to make his escape on foot, only to be overtaken and
killed by the warriors.

FIGURE 41

"It was a single Indian who killed the head packer
and captured two mules loaded with ammunition,
but could not hold them lone-handed."
—Camille Williams to Lucullus McWhorter

Again, blue pencil outlines define most shapes, with red and blue pencil used for fill-in. The red-shirted warrior Ɂiceyeye Pewwetes literally strikes again. This time his wrath is directed at what seems to be a member of Howard's pack train during the Clearwater engagement. Howard's civilian packer was apparently riding the long-eared red mule seen running just ahead of him.[124] A bedroll and a canteen are shown attached to the mule's saddle. Though armed with a pistol, this packer seems more concerned with making good his getaway than defending himself. Blood ominously pours from his wounded head. Blue dashed lines in the background represent either bullets or the speed of the action. The white man's hat is unusual in that it resembles the old military "dragoon" style of the 1850s and earlier.

Ɂiceyeye, for he is almost certainly this red-shirted figure, must truly go down in Nez Perce records as a courageous and formidable warrior. To engage in hand-to-hand fighting with a hatchet not just once but numerous times shows the confidence this man had in his personal spirit power and makes clear his determination to protect his family and friends from the soldiers' aggression.

FIGURE 42

"The Indian flankers by their rapid movement struck the rear of the small (pack) train, killed two of the packers and disabled a couple of mules loaded with howitzer ammunition. The prompt fire from Perry's and Whipple's cavalry saved the ammunition from capture."
—O. O. Howard

Blue pencil lines delineate most of the shapes, with blue and red pencil used to fill in the shapes. Layering of colors gave the artist more variety in hues. Seen through the blue of the blanket capote is the top half of the warrior's red legging, drawn prior to the capote in order to obtain the correct pose and proportions for the figure. "Soldier" is written in India ink.

Another unfortunate packer tries to make his getaway on a long-eared mule, dutifully driving a loaded pack mule before him. The blue-capoted warrior, possibly Laʔamninnim Husus again, closes in armed with what appears to be a model 1873 single-action Colt. The packer also has a pistol, worn in a right-handed cross-draw position. Blue dashes may imply bullets or the speed of the chase. Use of this heavy blanket capote seems unusual in light of reports that the "thermometer was somewhere around the 100 mark" during this day of fighting.[125] Picturing this individual wearing his capote may be the artist's way of helping viewers identify him by association with a familiar item of his dress, even if he wasn't wearing the capote during the fight. Also recall that warriors occasionally tied their war medicine to their capotes (see figures 31 and 36). This warrior may have had his medicine tied to this capote, hidden from view in this drawing, and regardless of the weather, chose to keep his spiritual power close to him. Going into battle without one's war medicine would ensure failure and invite death.

The artist had a wonderful eye and memory for detail. The full bushy beard of this packer would almost certainly identify him to any of his acquaintances. Also notice the detail of his nonmilitary iron stirrups and spurs.

102   The *Cash Book* Drawings

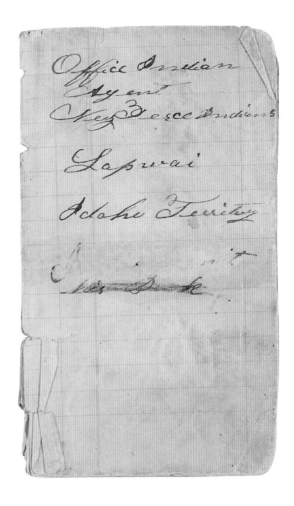

FIGURE 43

The writing is in India ink, with some words erased and others crossed out with red and blue pencil. "Office Indian Agent, Nez Perce Indians, Lapwai, Idaho Territory [erasure], his Book." Were these erased words the same as those erased in figure 25? Remnants of writing left on both pages show similar pen strokes. Continued research may some day reveal whose name or title belongs in this space.

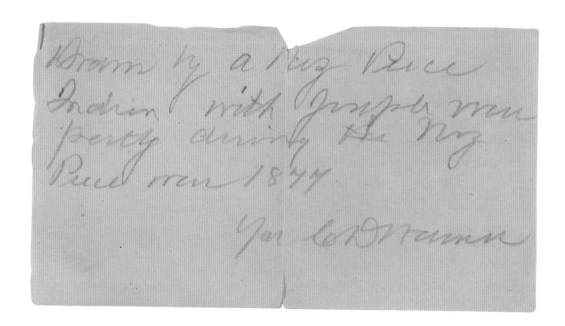

FIGURE 44. INSERT

"Drawn by a Nez Perce Indian with Joseph war party during the Nez Perce war 1877. Maj. C. D. Warner."

Graphite pencil was used to produce this note written by Agent Charles D. Warner and enclosed within the *Cash Book*. Warner, realizing the importance of this little book, preserved it and passed it along together with his papers.

FIGURE 45. REAR ENDPAPER

Two capital letters, M and S, are in India ink. After the S, the remainder of the word "Saman" (salmon) has been written in graphite pencil. Apparently the writer made use of the already written S to form the word "Saman." Drawings are outlined with what seems to be graphite pencil rather than black colored pencil. Red and blue pencils were used to fill in the shapes.

Little birds perch on a delicately leafed limb. A salmon, one of the major food sources of the "downriver" Nez Perce such as the Wallowa band, is shown. If the drawings in the *Cash Book* were sequenced front to back, the story opens with a picture of a bison, the food from the Plains, and concludes with a salmon, the traditional staple of the Plateau people.

FIGURE 46. BACK COVER

Calfskin. The back cover has no definite distinguishing marks except for a faint circle, the same diameter as the one on the front cover.

There is no doubt as to the ethnographic value of the drawings contained in the *Cash Book*. Because of the artist's careful attention to detail in clothing and accouterments, we have a visual record of the styles of dress and equipment in common use among those who were known as the nontreaty Nez Perce. Designs painted on the covers of warriors' shields, cougar furs draped over horses' backs as ornamental padding for riders in the parades, and symbolic head feathers selected from a variety of birds are all part of the rich material culture displayed by the nontreaty Nez Perce of the 1870s and presented by the *Cash Book* artist. Instead of being trapped behind museum glass exhibited as disconnected objects, these material items are shown in the *Cash Book* drawings as they were used in daily life and incorporated into a person's outfit. The drawings contribute to an understanding of the ornamentation required by spiritual beliefs and also reveal some of the aesthetic tastes of individuals. And they emphasize the extent to which items of white manufacture became part of traditional Nez Perce material culture—blankets for men's leggings, rolled-fringe shawls tailored for use as breechcloths, cloth dresses trimmed with colorful ribbons, and iron bits with commercially tanned leather bridles. Even the drawings themselves, focusing on Native people and events that altered their lives, seem influenced by white pictorial communications and perspective techniques.

In contrast to the ease of analyzing elements of Nez Perce material culture clearly shown in the drawings is the difficulty of having to make assumptions regarding the identity of some of the individuals pictured, and of the events being shown. Fortunately, the *Cash Book* drawings provide enough clues that the number of assumptions possible about the artist's intentions for certain drawings can be narrowed greatly.

Though none of the information so far interpreted from the *Cash Book* drawings is so unique that history will have to be rewritten as a result, the drawings do confirm pictorially much of what other sources, especially the works of Lucullus McWhorter, present in written form.

The truly special aspect of the *Cash Book* drawings is their focus on individuals who have been unknown or largely overlooked by white historians. Without a drawing, few would have been able to visualize the efforts of footless Itskimzekin bravely fighting beside his adoptive Nez Perce people from shallow depressions along the Big Hole River with a six-shooter, probably the only weapon available to him at the time. Or one of the many exploits credited to Piyopyo Talikt, his duel with the Cheyenne at the Bear Paw battlefield. ʔiceyeye Pewwetes, mentioned only briefly in McWhorter's works, is shown to be among the most determined and fearless of the warriors during the attack on a pack train. It can certainly be imagined that ʔiceyeye was no less resolute during other engagements.

Finally, a man named Laʔamninnim Husus is brought to light. His name appears more than any other throughout the *Cash Book*—ten times. Like Piyopyo and ʔiceyeye, his identity is associated with others of the young warrior class. And what may be most significant of all is the possibility that Laʔamninnim Husus was the *Cash Book* artist who left for us, through the preservation efforts of agent Charles Warner and Mary Beck and her family, a wealth of artistic and ethnographic information. Laʔamninnim is the most likely person to have been the artist who preserved, for historians and descendants, the images of many veterans of the 1877 war who until now have been known only in Nez Perce oral history.

Notes

1. Lessard, "Plains Pictographic Art," 62. In the case of the *Cash Book*, military "culture" is also represented.

2. Walker, *Conflict and Schism*, 14. Walker writes that bands who stayed at home, who depended on roots and salmon, were labeled with a derogatory term roughly meaning "provincials," while the bison hunters referred to themselves as "sophisticated people."

3. Peopeo Tholekt, cage 55, box 9-A, 1927, "Battle of the Big Hole, Nez Perce Camp," Washington State University Libraries, Pullman; McWhorter Papers, cage 55, folder 161, n.d.; Andrew Garcia, *Tough Trip through Paradise* (Boston: Houghton Mifflin, 1967), 238.

4. McWhorter Papers, cage 55, folder 170, n.d., "Narrative of Red Elk."

5. Aoki, *Nez Perce Dictionary*, 1120.

6. McWhorter, *Yellow Wolf*, 290.

7. Cora Dubois, *The Feather Cult of the Middle Columbia Salish* (Menasha: George Banta, 1938), 39; Shawley, interview, 15 June 1992.

8. Spier, *Prophet Dance*, 43.

9. Dubois, *Feather Cult*, 14; Mooney, *Ghost Dance Religion*; Spier, *Prophet Dance*, 442, 445.

10. Click Relander, *Drummers and Dreamers* (Caldwell: Caxton, 1956), 84.

11. O. B. Sperlin, "Exploration of the Upper Columbia," *Washington Historical Quarterly* 4, no. 4 (January 1913): 3–11; Ella E. Clark, *Indian Legends from the Northern Rockies* (Norman: University of Oklahoma Press, 1966), 34; McWhorter, *Yellow Wolf*, 42. Significance of the number three could have roots in, or gained emphasis from, Christian missionaries' teachings regarding the Holy Trinity, see Jay Miller's Introduction in Mourning Dove, *Coyote Stories* (Lincoln: University of Nebraska Press, 1990), xii–xiii; Dubois, *Feather Cult*, 40; Spier, *Prophet Dance*, 30, 46. The numbers five and seven were also important in Nez Perce spirituality.

12. Dubois, *Feather Cult*, 13; Relander, *Drummers and Dreamers*, 71, 82, 154.

13. Eugene S. Hunn, *Nch'i-Wána: "The Big River"* (Seattle: University of Washington Press, 1990), 257.

14. Halfmoon, interview, 15 August 1992; Peters, interview, 19 June 1993; Shawley, interview, 15 June 1992.

15. Relander, *Drummers and Dreamers*, 71, 154, 155; Mooney, *Ghost-Dance Religion*, 727; Dubois, *Feather Cult*, 17.

16. Gladys Reichard, *An Analysis of Coeur d'Alene Indian Myths* (Philadelphia: American Folklore Society, 1947), 75, 76; Spier, *Prophet Dance*, 43.

17. Deward Walker, Jr., "Nez Perce Sorcery," in *Systems of North American Witchcraft and Sorcery*, ed. Deward Walker, Jr. (Moscow: University of Idaho, 1970), 282.

18. Axtell, interview, 7 August 1994.

19. Relander, *Drummers and Dreamers*, 71.

20. Hunn, *Nch'i Wána*, 234; Relander, *Drummers and Dreamers*, 156; Spier *Prophet Dance*, 7, 8.

21. Hunn, *Nch'i-Wána*, 255; Relander, *Drummers and Dreamers*, 70–74.

22. Peters, interview, 19 June 1993; Relander, *Drummers and Dreamers*, 84, figure 1.

23. Dubois, *Feather Cult*, 18.

24. George Hatley to author, 8 September 1993.

25. Lavender, *Let Me Be Free*, 287.

26. McWhorter, *Yellow Wolf*, 75–79.

27. Alvin Josephy to author, 7 January 1994; Peters, interview, 19 June 1993; Shawley, "Nez Perce Dress," 231; McWhorter, *Hear Me*, 471; McWhorter, *Yellow Wolf*, 93, 303; Merriam, *Flathead Indian Music*, 78, 83.

28. Alvin M. Josephy, *The Nez Perce Indians and the Opening of the West* (1965; New York: Houghton Mifflin, 1997), 576–77; "Nez Perce Camp"; McWhorter, *Yellow Wolf* (quotation), 110.

29. Roger Ernesti, personal interview, 14 August 1992; Peters, interview, 19 June 1993.

30. *Chief Joseph and Warriors Memorial Celebration*, 6; Steven D. Shawley, personal interview, 4 August 1982.

31. Josephy to author, 7 January 1994; McWhorter, *Yellow Wolf*, 120.

32. Shawley, interview, 9 November 1991; John C. Ewers, "Nicolas Point's Paintings of Flathead Indians," paper delivered to the Eastern Washington State Historical Society, Spokane, 10 October 1989; Ronald McCoy, "Circles of Power," *Plateau*, 1984, 1–32; Spinden, 227.

33. Ewers, *The Horse*, 97; Richard Kuh, "Achievement Marks of the Plains Indians," *Powder Burns*, April 1983, 1.

34. Ewers, *The Horse*, 100; Marquis, *Memoirs of a White Crow Indian*, 114.

35. Erasmas D. Keyes, *Fighting Indians in Washington Territory* (Fairfield: Ye Galleon, 1988), 25; "Blanket, horse," Nez Perce National Historic Park, catalog no. 2304, Spalding, Idaho; Ewers *The Horse*, 94–95.

36. Shawley, "Nez Perce Dress," 86, 261; Nettie Shawaway, personal interview, 6 August 1982.

37. Shawley, "Nez Perce Dress," 95. Also see *Animal People: Teacher's Guide* (Seattle: Daybreak Star, n.d.), 5. The true origin and antiquity of the term "wing dress" is one of a number of topics in need of more study.

38. Spinden, *Nez Perce Indians*, 224. Spinden's work on the Nez Perce has several surprising gaps in its information, including statements such as "It is not known how women's leggings differ from those of the men" (217), and "No information regarding . . . vegetable dyes could be obtained" (222). It is possible that he also failed to gain accurate information on the use of tattoos. Tattooing of arms and hands was practiced by other Plateau people. See Verne F. Ray, *Culture Element Distribution: Plateau* (Berkeley: University of California Press, 1942), 171.

39. McWhorter, *Hear Me*, 394, 561; Joseph, *Chief Joseph: His Own Story* (Fairfield: Ye Galleon, 1984), 25.

40. McWhorter Papers, cage 55, folder 160, "Last Battle"; cage 55, folder 170, "Red Wolf's Narrative."

41. McWhorter, *Yellow Wolf*, 133.

42. An interviewee's statement to Caroline James, *Nez Perce Women in Transition, 1877–1990* (Moscow: University of Idaho Press, 1996), 215.

43. McWhorter, *Yellow Wolf*, and Joseph, *Chief Joseph*, 20.

44. McWhorter, *Hear Me*, 43.

45. McWhorter, *Yellow Wolf*, 126; *Hear Me*, 386. An in-depth discussion of a "war mate" partnership can be found in Carling Malouf's "Institutionalized Friendship Among Northern Plains and Plateau Indians," *Lifeways of Intermontane and Plains Montana Indians*, ed. Leslie B. Davis (Bozeman: Montana State University, 1979), 73–80.

46. Hunn, *Nch'i-Wána*, 61; John Reed Swanton, *Indian Tribes of Washington, Oregon, and Idaho* (1952; Fairfield: Ye Galleon, 1979), 4; Axtell, interview, 7 August 1994.

47. Howard, *Nez Perce Joseph*, 52.

48. Sue Emory (Director, Appaloosa Museum and Heritage Center Foundation) to author, 10 September 1993; Bill and Dona Richardson, *The Appaloosa* (South Brunswick: A. S. Barnes, 1969), 37; D. Phillip Sponenberg and Bonnie V. Beaver, *Horse Color* (College Station: Texas A&M University, 1983), 33, 103. For a pictographic sample of a curly haired horse, see Stern, Schmitt, and Halfmoon, "A Cayuse–Nez Perce Sketchbook," 367.

49. Jack R. Williams, "Nez Perce Horses: Their Controversy and Their History," *Appaloosa World*, June 1982, 37; Spinden, *Nez Perce Indians*, 29; Francis Haines, *Appaloosa* (Austin: University of Texas, 1963), 84, and again in *The Nez Perces* (Norman: University of Oklahoma Press, 1955), 23.

50. For additional thoughts on the historic popularity of Appaloosas among the Nez Perce, see Williams, *Appaloosa World*, June 1982, 34–43, and July 1982, 31–44; Debbie Pitner Moors, "Range Bred and Born," *Appaloosa Journal*, January 1987, 76, 77. Some of the horses pictured in the *Cash Book* were undoubtedly non-Appaloosas acquired from whites later in the war to replace tired or injured Indian horses, thus further decreasing the percentage of Appaloosas available to be pictured.

51. McWhorter, *Hear Me*, 283, 373, 388; *Yellow Wolf*, 295; June Randolph, "Witness of Indian Religion: Present-day Concepts of the Guardian Spirit," *Pacific Northwest Quarterly*, October 1957, 140.

52. Shawley, interview, 4 August 1982.

53. McWhorter, *Hear Me*, 373.

54. Peters, interview, 19 June 1933.

55. Ernesti, interview, 14 August 1992; Jumping Bull, interview by Richard Kuh, 16 July 1992; Young Bear, interview by Richard Kuh, 17 July 1992.

56. This hair style was recognized as being so characteristic of the Lakota that the more westerly tribes even incorporated gestures into the rather universal sign language to indicate the "Sioux" custom of "parting the hair in the middle and combing it down over the sides of the head." William P. Clark, *The Indian Sign Language* (1885; Lincoln: University of Nebraska Press, 1982), 341.

57. Jumping Bull, interview, 16 July 1992; Young Bear, interview, 17 July 1992; Lynn Pankonin (Curator of Native American Collections, Cheney Cowles Museum, Spokane), personal interview, 11 August 1993.

58. Jumping Bull, interview, 16 July 1992.

59. McWhorter, *Hear Me*, 513.

60. James Walsh letter, Glenbow Museum Archives,

Calgary, Alberta, D364.971 W225.

61. McWhorter, *Hear Me*, 513–14.

62. McWhorter Papers, cage 55, folder 167, "Peopeo Tholekt's Narrative."

63. This scenario was suggested by Jumping Bull, interview, 16 July 1992. Also see Petersen, *Plains Indian Art*, 270, 274.

64. McWhorter, *Yellow Wolf*, 233–35.

65. For more details on the Sun Dance see Helen Blish, *A Pictographic History of the Oglala Sioux* (Lincoln: University of Nebraska Press, 1967), 91; Richard Erdoes, *Lame Deer: Seeker of Visions* (New York: Pocket Books, 1976), 193; Leslie Spier, "The Sun Dance of the Plains Indians: Its Development and Diffusion," *Anthropological Papers of the American Museum of Natural History* 16, pt. 7 (1921), and Densmore, *Teton Sioux Music*, 118, 122b, 132a.

66. Blish, *Pictographic History*, 93, 94.

67. Jumping Bull, interview, 16 July 1992.

68. Blish, *Pictographic History*, 591; Densmore, *Teton Sioux Music*, 130; Jumping Bull, interview, 16 July 1992; Young Bear, interview, 17 July 1992. Alternative ways of conducting the Sun Dance ceremony are discussed in Densmore, 87, Spier, "The Sun Dance of the Plains Indians," 464, 466, 473, and Joseph Epes Brown, *The Sacred Pipe* (Baltimore: Penguin Books, 1971), 93.

69. Harry Holbert Turney-High, *Ethnography of the Kutenai* (Menasha: American Anthropological Association, 1941), 169, offers the explanation that outfit exchanges enabled foreign or visiting tribes to become familiar with the host tribe's appearance. Another motive for outfit exchanges, generosity, albeit for the enhancement of one's personal or tribal status, was, and still is, a virtue among people of the Plains and Northwest. For further information on this topic, see Garcia, *Tough Trip*, 14; Gillette Griswold, "Aboriginal Patterns of Trade Between the Columbia Basin and the Northern Plains" (master's thesis, Montana State University, 1954), 120; Stanley Vestal, *Warpath* (1934; Lincoln: University of Nebraska Press, 1984), 22–23. Also note that in the collection of the National Park Service, Big Hole National Battlefield Historic Site, there is a Lakota dress which is said to have belonged to Mrs. White Bird. Clothing exchange certainly seems to have occurred among the refugees in Canada.

70. Dubois, *Feather Cult*, 44.

71. Blish, *Pictographic History*, 65; Brown, *Sacred Pipe*, 69; Erdoes, *Lame Deer*, 194. Black Elk did, however, explain to Brown (*Sacred Pipe*, 7, 80) that the number seven does have some significance in the Lakota religion.

72. Jumping Bull, interview, 16 July 1992; Reginald Laubin and Gladys Laubin, *The Indian Tipi* (Norman: University of Oklahoma Press, 1957), 40–53, 173.

73. McWhorter, *Hear Me*, 515.

74. McWhorter, *Yellow Wolf*, 102, 111; Hampton, *Children of Grace*, 161.

75. Although a front view of a human subject in Native pictorial art is not unusual, in this case the front view is drawn in order to show regalia and accouterments to aid the viewer in identifying the subject. Hips and legs shown in a side view often suggest the subject's direction of action or attention. This portrait, however, offers an organized, detailed composition worthy of note, created as much for aesthetic effect as for recording action or exploits.

76. A full description of these weapons can be found in McWhorter, *Yellow Wolf*, 300a, 301, and in Spinden, *Nez Perce Indians*, 226.

77. Ella McCarty, personal interview, 19 February 1978; Shawley, interview, 10 November 1991.

78. McWhorter, *Yellow Wolf*, 51, 199.

79. Bartlett, *Wallowa Country*, 54.

80. Note the similarity, in form and decoration, of this bag to a Crow tobacco bag pictured in David W. Penney, *Art of the American Indian Frontier* (Seattle: University of Washington Press, 1992), 201, pl. 128. Artistic styles and trading relationships between the Crow and Nez Perce are topics of ongoing study and debate.

81. Phillip Katcher, in *The American Indian Wars: 1860–1890* (London: Osprey, 1977), 33, calls this style of shirt a "Hickory" shirt.

82. McWhorter, *Hear Me*, 540–41; *Yellow Wolf*, 292.

83. McWhorter, *Hear Me*, 509, 510.

84. Duncan McDonald, "The Nez Perces," 272.

85. Vestal, *Sitting Bull*, 153–54. Owhi, of Yakama heritage, was traveling and fighting with the Nez Perce. He describes his and Yellow Wolf's encounter with these helpful Indians: "In the morning on the north side of the Milk River we found a camp of Indians that looked as if they were part white. We caught one of their men . . .

he told us that three days before, Nez Perce had passed through there so we followed their trail." McWhorter Papers, cage 55, folder 172, "Owhi's Narrative."

86. McWhorter, *Yellow Wolf*, 234–35; *Hear Me*, 513.

87. Clark, in *Indian Sign Language*, describes signs for "bring," "chief," "come," and "disarm" which are similar to the sign the presumed Lakota may be making and all of which could relate to the first meeting of the Nez Perce and the Lakota. Also see signs in William Tomkins, *Indian Sign Language* (New York: Dover, 1969), for "alive," "alone," "chief," "come," "friend," "now," and "one."

88. Lawrence Kip, *Indian Council at Walla Walla* (Seattle: Shorey Book Store, 1971, rpt.), 11; Haines, *Nez Perces*, 102.

89. McWhorter, *Hear Me*, 104–5.

90. Peters, interview, 19 June 1993; Peopeo Tolekt, "Battle of the Big Hole, Nez Perce Camp," 1927.

91. McWhorter, *Hear Me*, 392; *Yellow Wolf*, 155–60.

92. This weapon, a modified 1868 Springfield, is pictured in McWhorter, *Yellow Wolf*, 132a. The caption wrongly identifies Walaytic's weapon as an Enfield rifle. Donald H. McTernan to author, 28 July 1994.

93. Terry Leaf to author, 26 November 1993.

94. McWhorter, *Yellow Wolf*, 132.

95. McWhorter, *Hear Me*, 392.

96. McWhorter, *Yellow Wolf*, 154.

97. McWhorter, *Hear Me*, 514.

98. Haines, *Nez Perces*, 51, 102; Lessard, "Plains Pictographic Art," 62–69, 90.

99. Peopeo Tholekt, "Battle of the Big Hole."

100. Collection information on "Wolf Hide Talisman," Catalog no. 8833, Nez Perce National Historic Park, Spalding, Idaho; McWhorter, *Yellow Wolf*, 154–55.

101. Katcher, *American Indian Wars*, 354; Leaf to author, 26 November 1993.

102. Tim O'Gorman to author, 14 September 1994; Dave Jurgella, personal interview, 7 August 1994; Leaf to author, 26 November 1993.

103. O'Gorman to author, 14 September 1994.

104. Shawley, "Nez Perce Dress," 192; *Chief Joseph and Warriors*, 3.

105. Blish, *Pictographic History*, 110; James A. Teit, *The Salishan Tribes of the Western Plateaus*, Bureau of American Ethnology, 45th Annual Report, 1927–28 (Washington, D.C.: Government Printing Office, 1930), 391.

106. Historian Alvin Josephy, who had an opportunity to study this drawing, had an impression similar to Halfmoon's and Peters's (above); Josephy to author, 7 January 1994.

107. Howard, *Report to the Secretary of War*, 603–6.

108. Katcher, *American Indian Wars*, 24–33; Leaf to author, 26 November 1993; O'Gorman to author, 14 September 1994.

109. Randy Steffen, *The Horse Soldier, 1776–1943* (Norman: University of Oklahoma, 1992), 2:103–5; Jurgella, interview, 8 August 1994; O'Gorman to author, 14 September 1994. The museum at the Big Hole Battlefield National Historical Park displays an "M. 1876 Prairie Belt," leather with canvas loops.

110. McWhorter, *Yellow Wolf*, 90.

111. McWhorter, *Hear Me*, 306.

112. McDonald, *Nez Perces*, 228, 235; Howard, *Nez Perce Joseph*, 1, 36.

113. Peopeo Tholekt, *Battle of the Big Hole*.

114. Piyopyo later explained, "After this engagement I learned from another of the enemy who threw to me the sign that they were not Sioux Indians but Cheyennes. That first man with the warbonnet fighting me told a lie! He was not a Sioux but a Cheyenne." McWhorter Papers, cage 55, folder 167, p. 15, "Peopeo Tholekt's Narrative."

115. McWhorter, *Hear Me*, 384.

116. Paqa Pantahank was spoken of by Yellow Wolf; it was said of Paqa, "he was of an old-time mind. He did not understand the gun. He was good with the bow, but had only a hunting bow. If he had a good gun, he could bring death to the soldiers."

117. McWhorter, *Yellow Wolf*, 122–23.

118. McWhorter, *Hear Me*, 303.

119. Robert Ruby and John A. Brown, *Indian Slavery in the Pacific Northwest* (Spokane: Arthur H. Clark, 1993), 232, 247.

120. McWhorter, *Yellow Wolf*, 53.

121. Brown, *Flight of the Nez Perce*, 380.

122. McWhorter, *Yellow Wolf*, 50, 53; *Hear Me*, 237.

123. Cyril B. Courville, "Trade Tomahawks" (Los Angeles: The Southwest Museum Leaflet Series, no. 30, 1963), 10–30.

124. Gillman and Pasha are names of two of the pack-

ers who met their end during the Clearwater fight, but
with fifty or more packers assigned to Howard's troops,
it is unlikely that the man pictured here will ever be positively identified. For further information on the use of
civilian packers see Brown, *Flight of the Nez Perce*, 152,
188–90, and Holterman, *The Eagle from the Rising Sun*, 7.

125. Brown, *Fight of the Nez Perce*, 190.

Bibliography

Alexander, Hartley B. "The Pictorial and Pictographic Art of the Indians of North America." *Cooke-Daniels Lectures.* Denver: Denver Art Museum, 1927.

Animal People: Teacher's Guide. Seattle: Daybreak Star, n.d.

Aoki, Haruo. *Nez Perce Dictionary.* Berkeley: University of California Press, 1994.

Bancroft, Hubert Howe. *The Works of Hubert Howe Bancroft*, vol. 31: *Washington, Idaho, and Montana, 1845–1889.* San Francisco: The History Company, 1890.

Bartlett, Grace. *The Wallowa Country, 1867–1877.* Fairfield, Wash.: Ye Galleon Press, 1984.

Beal, Merrill D. *"I Will Fight No More Forever": Chief Joseph and the Nez Perce War.* Seattle: University of Washington Press, 1963.

Biographical and Historical Index of American Indians and Persons Involved in Indian Affairs. Boston: G. K. Hall, 1966.

Blish, Helen H. *A Pictographic History of the Oglala Sioux.* Lincoln: University of Nebraska Press, 1967.

Brown, Joseph Epes. *The Sacred Pipe: Black Elk's Account of the Seven Rites of the Oglala Sioux.* Norman: University of Oklahoma Press, 1953.

Brown, Mark H. *The Flight of the Nez Perce.* Lincoln: University of Nebraska Press, 1967.

Carter, John. *ABC for Book Collectors.* New York: Alfred A. Knopf, 1951.

Chief Joseph and Warriors Memorial Celebration. Lapwai, Idaho: Chief Joseph and Warriors Memorial Celebration Committee, 1983.

Clark, Ella E. *Indian Legends from the Northern Rockies.* Norman: University of Oklahoma Press, 1966.

Clark, William P. *The Indian Sign Language.* Reprint. Lincoln: University of Nebraska Press, 1982.

Courville, Cyril B. "Trade Tomahawks." Los Angeles: The Southwest Museum Leaflet Series, no. 30, 1963.

Densmore, Frances. *Teton Sioux Music.* Bureau of American Ethnology Bulletin 61. Washington, D.C.: Government Printing Office, 1918.

Drury, Clifford M. *Chief Lawyer of the Nez Perce Indians, 1796–1876.* Glendale, Calif.: Arthur H. Clark, 1979.

Dubois, Cora. *The Feather Cult of the Middle Columbia*

Salish. General Series in Anthropology, no. 7. Menasha, Wisc.: George Banta, 1938.

Dunn, Dorothy. *American Indian Painting of the Southwest and Plains Areas*. Albuquerque: University of New Mexico, 1968.

Erdoes, Richard. *Lame Deer: Seeker of Visions*. New York: Pocket Books, 1976.

Ewers, John C. *The Horse in Blackfoot Indian Culture*. Washington, D.C.: Smithsonian Institution Press, 1955, 1980.

——. *Plains Indian Painting*. Stanford: Stanford University Press, 1939.

Fawcett, David M., and Lee A. Callander. *Native American Painting*. New York: Museum of the American Indian, 1982.

Feest, Christian F. *Native Arts of North America*. New York: Oxford University Press, 1980.

Fitzgerald, Emily. *An Army Doctor's Wife on the Frontier*. Pittsburgh: University of Pittsburgh Press, 1962.

Furst, Peter T., and Jill L. Furst. *North American Indian Art*. New York: Artpress, 1982.

Garcia, Andrew. *Tough Trip Through Paradise, 1878–1879*. Boston: Houghton Mifflin, 1967.

Goldin, Theodore. *A Bit of the Nez Perce Campaign*. Bryan, Texas: Theodore Goldin, 1978.

Haines, Francis. *Appaloosa*. Austin: University of Texas, 1963.

——. *The Nez Perces*. Norman: University of Oklahoma Press, 1955.

Hampton, Bruce. *Children of Grace: The Nez Perce War of 1877*. New York: Henry Holt, 1994.

Hawley, James H. *History of Idaho: The Gem of the Mountains*. Chicago: S. J. Clarke, 1920.

Hines, Donald M. *Ghost Voices*. Issaquah, Wash.: Great Eagle, 1992.

Holterman, Jack. *The Eagle from the Rising Sun*. West Glacier: Glacier Natural History Association, 1991.

Howard, Helen Addison. *Saga of Chief Joseph*. Caldwell, Idaho: Caxton, 1965.

Howard, O. O. *Nez Perce Joseph*. Boston: Lee and Shepard, 1881.

Hunn, Eugene S. *Nch'i-Wána: "The Big River."* Seattle: University of Washington Press, 1990.

Irving, Washington. *Adventures of Captain Bonneville, U.S.A., in the Rocky Mountains and the Far West*. Norman: University of Oklahoma Press, 1961.

James, Caroline. *Nez Perce Women in Transition, 1877–1990*. Moscow: University of Idaho Press, 1996.

Joseph. *Chief Joseph: His Own Story*. Fairfield, Wash.: Ye Galleon Press, 1984.

Josephy, Alvin M. *Chief Joseph's People and Their War*. Yellowstone National Park: The Yellowstone Association, 1964.

——. *The Nez Perce Indians and the Opening of the Northwest*. New Haven: Yale University Press, 1965. New York: Houghton Mifflin, 1997.

Katcher, Phillip, and G. A. Embleton. *The American Indian Wars: 1860–1890*. London: Osprey, 1977.

Keyes, Erasmas D. *Fighting Indians in Washington Territory*. Fairfield: Ye Galleon Press, 1988.

Kip, Lawrence. *Indian Council at Walla Walla*. Reprint. Seattle: Shorey Book Store, 1971.

Laubin, Reginald, and Gladys Laubin. *The Indian Tipi*. Norman: University of Oklahoma Press, 1957.

Lavender, David. *Let Me Be Free: The Nez Perce Tragedy*. New York: HarperCollins, 1992.

Manzione, Joseph. *"I Am Looking to the North for My Life": Sitting Bull, 1876–1881*. Salt Lake City: University of Utah Press, 1991.

Marquis, Thomas B. *Memoirs of a White Crow Indian (Thomas H. Leforge)*. Lincoln: University of Nebraska Press, 1974.

McBeth, Kate. *The Nez Perces Since Lewis and Clark*. New York: F. H. Revell, 1908. Moscow: University of Idaho Press, 1993.

McDermott, John D. *Forlorn Hope: The Battle of White Bird Canyon and the Beginning of the Nez Perce War*. Boise: Idaho State Historical Society, 1978.

McDonald, Duncan. "The Nez Perces: The History of Their Troubles and the Campaign of 1877." In *In Pursuit of the Nez Perces*, compiled by Linwood Laughy. Wrangell, Alaska: Mountain Meadow Press, 1993.

McDowell, R. Bruce. *Evolution of the Winchester*, Tacoma, Wash.: Armory, 1985.

McWhorter, Lucullus. *Hear Me, My Chiefs!: Nez Perce History and Legend*. Caldwell, Idaho: Caxton, 1952, 1983, 1986.

———. *Yellow Wolf: His Own Story*. Caldwell, Idaho: Caxton, 1940, 1983.

Merriam, Alan P., and Barbara Merriam. *Flathead Indian Music*. Missoula: Montana State University School of Music, 1950.

Mooney, James. *The Ghost-Dance Religion and the Sioux Outbreak of 1890*. Bureau of American Ethnology, 14th Annual Report, pt. 2, pp. 641–1136. Washington, D.C.: Government Printing Office, 1896.

Morvillo, Anthony. *A Dictionary of the Numipu or Nez Perce Language*. St. Ignatius, Mont.: St. Ignatius Mission, 1895.

Mourning Dove. *Coyote Stories*. Lincoln: University of Nebraska Press, 1990.

"Nez Perce Camp: Big Hole National Battlefield." n.p.: Yellowstone Library and Museum Association, 1977.

Nez Perce Country. Washington, D.C.: U.S. Department of the Interior, National Park Service, 1983.

Petersen, Karen D. *Plains Indian Art from Fort Marion*. Norman: University of Oklahoma Press, 1971.

Phillips, Paul C., ed. "The Battle of the Big Hole." *Sources of North West History*, no. 8. Missoula: State University of Montana, n.d.

Point, Nicolas, S.J. *Wilderness Kingdom*. Chicago: Loyola University Press, 1967.

Ray, Verne F. *Cultural Element Distribution: Plateau*. Berkeley: University of California Press, 1942.

———. *Cultural Relations in the Plateau of Northwestern America*. Los Angeles: The Southwest Museum, 1939.

———. "Ethnohistory of the Joseph Band of Nez Perce Indians: 1805–1905." In *Nez Perce Indians*. New York: Garland, 1974.

Relander, Click. *Drummers and Dreamers*. Caldwell, Idaho: Caxton, 1956.

Richardson, Bill, and Dona Richardson. *The Appaloosa*. South Brunswick, N.J.: A. S. Barnes, 1969.

Ross, Alexander. *Adventures of the First Settlers on the Oregon or Columbia River*. London: Smith, Elder, and Company, 1849.

———. *The Fur Hunters of the Far West*. Norman: University of Oklahoma Press, 1956.

Ross, John A. "Political Conflict on the Colville Reservation." *Northwest Anthropological Research Notes* 2, no. 1 (1968): 29–91.

Ruby, Robert H., and John A. Brown. *The Cayuse Indians*. Norman: University of Oklahoma Press, 1979.

———. *Indian Slavery in the Pacific Northwest*. Spokane, Wash.: Arthur H. Clark Co., 1993.

Shields, George O. *The Battle of the Big Hole*. Chicago: Rand, McNally, 1889.

Spier, Leslie. *The Prophet Dance of the Northwest and Its Derivatives: The Source of the Ghost Dance*. Menasha, Wisc.: George Banta, 1935.

———. "The Sun Dance of the Plains Indians: Its Development and Diffusion." *Anthropological Papers of the American Museum of Natural History* 16, pt. 7 (1921).

Spinden, Herbert J. *The Nez Perce Indians*. Lancaster, Penn.: New Era, 1908.

Sponenberg, D. Phillip, and Bonnie V. Beaver. *Horse Color*. College Station: Texas A&M University, 1983.

Steffan, Randy. *The Horse Soldier, 1776–1943*. Norman: University of Oklahoma Press, vol. 2, 1992.

Suttles, Wayne. "Plateau Pacifism Reconsidered—Ethnography, Ethnology, and Ethnohistory." In *Coast Salish Essays*, 282–86. Seattle: University of Washington Press, 1987.

Swanton, John Reed. *Indian Tribes of Washington, Oregon, and Idaho*. Reprint of 1952 report. Fairfield, Wash.: Ye Galleon Press, 1979.

Teit, James A. *The Salishan Tribes of the Western Plateaus*. Bureau of American Ethnology, 45th Annual Report, 1927–28, pp. 23–396. Washington, D.C.: Government Printing Office, 1930.

Thompson, Erwin N. *Historic Resource Study: Spalding Area*. Denver: U.S. Department of the Interior, National Park Service, 1972.

Tomkins, William. *Indian Sign Language*. Reprint of fifth edition, 1931. New York: Dover, 1969.

Trafzer, Clifford E., and Richard D. Scheuerman. *Chief Joseph's Allies: The Palouse Indians and the Nez Perce War of 1877*. Sacramento: Sierra Oaks, 1987.

———. *Renegade Tribe*. Pullman: Washington State University Press, 1986.

Turner, John Peter. *The North-West Mounted Police, 1873–1893*. Ottawa: Edmond Cloutier/King's Printer, 1950.

Turney-High, Harry Holbert. *Ethnography of the Kutenai*. Menasha, Wisc.: American Anthropological Association, 1941.

Utley, Robert M. *Frontier Regulars: The United States Army and the Indian, 1866–1891*. New York: Macmillan, 1973.

Vestal, Stanley, *Sitting Bull: Champion of the Sioux*. Norman: University of Oklahoma Press, 1957.

——. *Warpath*. Boston: Houghton Mifflin, 1934. Lincoln: University of Nebraska Press, 1984.

Walker, Deward E., Jr. *Indians of Idaho*. Anthropological Monographs, no. 2, Moscow: University of Idaho, 1978.

——. *Conflict and Schism in Nez Perce Acculturation*. Moscow: University of Idaho Press, 1985.

——. "Nez Perce Sorcery." *Systems of North American Witchcraft and Sorcery*. Edited by Deward Walker, Jr. Moscow: University of Idaho, 1970.

Wilson, Bruce A. *From Where the Sun Now Stands*. Omak, Wash.: Omak Chronicle, 1960.

Wissler, Clark. *Indian Cavalcade, or Life on the Old-Time Indian Reservations*. New York: Sheridan House, 1938.

PERIODICALS AND NEWSPAPERS

Anastasio, Angelo. "Southern Plateau: An Ecological Analysis of Intergroup Relations." *Northwest Anthropological Research Notes* 2 (Fall 1972): 109–228.

Coeur d'Alene Press, 27 March 1920.

Geyer, Charles A. "Notes on the Vegetation and General Character of the Missouri and Oregon Territories, Made during a Botanical Journey from the State of Missouri, across the South Pass of the Rocky Mountains, to the Pacific, during the years 1843 and 1844." *London Journal of Botany* 5 (1845–46): 509–24.

Greene, Candace S. "Artists in Blue: The Indian Scouts of Fort Reno and Fort Supply." *American Indian Art*, Winter 1992, 50–57.

Gunther, Erna. "The Westward Movement of Some Plains Traits." *American Anthropologist* 52, no. 2 (1950): 174–80.

Johnson, Michael. "The Influence of Plains Material Culture on the Plateau Tribes." *Pow Wow Trails*, November 1967, 4–6.

Kuh, Richard. "Achievement Marks of the Plains Indians." *Powder Burns*, April 1983, 1.

Lessard, F. Dennis. "Plains Pictographic Art: A Source of Ethnographic Information." *American Indian Art*, Spring 1992, 62–69, 90.

McCoy, Ronald. "Circles of Power." *Plateau*, 1984, 1–32.

Moors, Debbie Pitner. "Range Bred and Born." *Appaloosa Journal*, January 1987, 72–77.

Packard, R. L. "Notes on the Mythology and Religion of the Nez Perces." *Journal of American Folklore* (1891): 327–30.

Ray, Verne F. "Native Villages and Groupings of the Columbia Basin." *Pacific Northwest Quarterly* 27, no. 2 (1936): 99–152.

Sperlin, O. B. "Exploration of the Upper Columbia." *Washington Historical Quarterly* 4, no. 4 (January 1913): 3–11.

Stern, Theodore, Martin Schmitt, and Alphonse F. Halfmoon. "A Cayuse–Nez Perce Sketchbook." *Oregon Historical Quarterly* 81, no. 4 (Winter 1980): 340–76.

Watters, Mari. "Seven Drum Religion Remains Important to Plateau Indians." *Response*, June 1985, 14–15, 35.

Williams, Jack R. "Nez Perce Horses: Their Controversy and Their History." *Appaloosa World*, June 1982, 34–43; July 1982, 31–44.

UNPUBLISHED SOURCES

J. M. Cornelison Papers. Cage 3007. Washington State University Libraries, Pullman, Washington. "A Dictionary of the Numipu or Nez Perce Language." n.d.

Eagle of the Light. "Speech of Eagle of the Light, 15 July 1881." Transcribed speech. Charles D. Warner Papers, Beck Family collection.

Griswold, Gillette. "Aboriginal Patterns of Trade Between the Columbia Basin and the Northern Plains." Master's thesis. Montana State University, 1954.

Kush, George. Photostatic copies of North-West Mounted Police records relating to the murder of White Bird. Viewed 7 August 1994.

McBeth, Susan Law. "A Nez Perce Dictionary." Manuscript. Washington State University, Pullman, Washington. Holland Library Archives, n.d.

L. V. McWhorter Papers. Cage 55. Washington State University Libraries, Pullman, Washington. Folder 160. "Last Battle." n.d.

Folder 161. Yellow Wolf to McWhorter. n.d.

Folder 163. "Killing of White Bird." n.d.

Folder 163. "Yellow Wolf, July 1926. Anecdotes of Chief Peo Peo Hi Hi: 'White Bird.'" 1926.

Folder 163. "Nez Perces Who Escaped to Canada and Never Were Captured." 1928.

Folder 167. "Peopeo Tholekt's Narrative." n.d.

Folder 170. "Narrative of Red Elk." n.d.

Folder 170. "Red Wolf's Narrative." n.d.

Folder 172. "Owhi's Narrative." n.d.

Folder 520. Yellow Wolf to McWhorter. n.d.

Monteith, Frances Whitman. "Indian Troubles and Treaties." Manuscript. Spokane Public Library, Spokane, Washington. North West Room, n.d.

Shawley, Steven D. "Nez Perce Dress: A Study in Cultural Change." Master's thesis. University of Idaho, 1974.

Shu-yai. "Speech of Shu-yai (Unpainted)." M. Beck Collection, 1881.

Walsh, James. "James Walsh to Cora Walsh, 1890." Calgary, Alberta. Glenbow Museum Archives. D 364.971 W 225.

GOVERNMENT DOCUMENTS

Gibbon, John. *Report to the Secretary of War*. Executive Documents, 45th Cong. 2d sess., 1877–1878. Washington, D.C.: Government Printing Office.

Howard, O. O. *Report to the Secretary of War*. Executive Documents, 45th Cong. 2d sess., 1877–1878. Washington, D.C.: Government Printing Office.

"Payroll Accounts, 1881, Nez Perce Agency, Lapwai, ID." Seattle: National Archives, Pacific Alaska Region (Seattle).

Warner, Charles D. "Lapwai Agency." *Annual Report of the Commissioner of Indian Affairs*. Executive Document I, p. 163. Washington, D.C.: Government Printing Office, 1879.

Warner, Charles D. Letter to E. A. Hayt, Commissioner of Indian Affairs, May 26, 1879. "Petition for return of Joseph's followers Now among the Sioux." National Archives, Collection RG 75. Microfilm Copy M 234, Roll 351, pp. 0569–0572. Records of the Bureau of Indian Affairs, 1879. P 104–w2625.

NONPRINT SOURCES

"Blanket, horse." Catalog no. 2304. Nez Perce National Historic Park, Spalding, Idaho.

Cullooya, Francis. "Spirituality and Sacred Ways." Lecture presented at Spokane Falls Community College, Spokane, Washington, 26 September 1992.

Ewers, John C. "Nicolas Point's Paintings of Flathead Indians." Lecture delivered at the Eastern Washington State Historical Society, Spokane, Washington, 10 October 1989.

Piyopyo Talikt. *Battle of the Big Hole, Nez Perce Camp*. Drawing. Cage 55. Washington State University, Pullman, Washington, Holland Library Archives.

The Real People: Legend of the Stick Game. Videocassette. Spokane: KSPS Television, 1976.

"Wolf Hide Talisman." Catalog no. 8833. Nez Perce National Historic Park, Spalding, Idaho.

INTERVIEWS AND CORRESPONDENCE

Axtell, Horace. Personal interview, 7 August 1994.

Beck, Mary. Personal interviews, 14 May 1992, 6 June 1992, 15 December 1992. Letter to author, 1 February 1993.

Clark, Bob. (Arthur H. Clark Co.) Personal interview, 2 July 1993.

Ellenwood, Richard. Personal interview, 7 August 1994.

Emory, Sue. (The Appaloosa Museum and Heritage Foundation.) Letter to author, 10 September 1993.

Ernesti, Roger. (Formerly of Roger Swaps Indian Store, Wapato, Washington.) Personal interview, 14 August 1992.

Ewers, John C. Letter to author, 22 January 1993.

Halfmoon, Nancy. Personal interview, 15 August 1992.

Hatley, George. Letter to author, 8 September 1993.

Jackson, Dorothy. Personal interviews, 15 August 1992, 8 January 1993.

Josephy, Alvin. Letter to author, 7 January 1994.

Jumping Bull, Calvin. Interview conducted by Richard Kuh, 16 July 1992.

Jurgella, Dave. (Big Hole National Battlefield.) Personal interview, 7 August 1994.

Justice, Joyce. (National Archives, Pacific Alaska Region [Seattle].) Letter to author, 22 February 1993.

Kush, George. Personal interview, 7 August 1994.

Leaf, Terry. Personal interview, 8 December 1993. Letter to author, 26 November 1993.

McCarty, Ella. Personal interview, 19 February 1978.

McTernan, Donald H. (Springfield Armory National Historic Site.) Letter to author, 28 July 1994.

O'Gorman, Tim. (U.S. Army Quartermaster Museum.) Letter to author, 14 September 1994.

Pankonin, Lynn. (Cheney Cowles Museum, Spokane, Washington.) Personal interview, 11 August 1993.

Peters, Kevin. (Nez Perce National Historic Park, Spalding Site.) Personal interview, 19 June 1993.

Peters, Kevin, and Horace Axtell. Letter to author, 27 October 1993.

Randall, Art. (Museum of North Idaho.) Letter to author, 13 January 1993.

Shawaway, Nettie. Personal interview, 6 August 1982.

Shawley, Steven D. Personal interviews, 4 August 1982, 9 November 1991, 10 November 1991. Telephone interview, 15 June 1992.

Stevenson, Lela. Personal interview, 31 August 1991.

Wright, Glenn. (Public Affairs and Information, Royal Canadian Mounted Police.) Letter to author, 16 January 1997.

Young Bear, Severt, Sr. Interview conducted by Richard Kuh, 17 July 1992.

Sources for Epigraphs in Captions

Cash Book figure indicated by boldface

Front cover: Mary Beck interview, 14 May 1992. **Front endpaper**: Nancy Halfmoon interview, 15 August 1992. **3**: Karen Petersen, *Plains Indian Art from Fort Madison*, 25. **4**: Kevin Peters interview, 19 June 1993. **5**: Steven D. Shawley interview, 15 June 1992. **6**: Mari Watters, "Seven Drum Religion Remains Important to Plateau Indians," 14. **7**: Cassius Day as quoted in McWhorter, *Hear Me*, 297. **8**: Nancy Halfmoon interview, 15 August 1992; Washington Irving, *Adventures of Captain Bonneville*, 79. **9**: Alexander Ross, *Adventures of the First Settlers on the Oregon or Columbia River*, 136. **10**: McWhorter, *Hear Me*, 312. **12**: Nancy Halfmoon interview, 15 August 1992. **13**: McWhorter, *Yellow Wolf*, 149–50. **14**: Ewers, *The Horse in Blackfoot Indian Culture*, 97. **15**: McWhorter, *Hear Me*, 374. **17**: Nancy Halfmoon interview, 15 August 1992. **18**: Calvin Jumping Bull interview by Richard Kuh, 16 July 1992. **20**: Ibid. **21**: Frances Densmore, *Teton Sioux Music*, 130. **23**: McWhorter, *Hear Me*, 371. **24**: Ewers to author, 22 January 1993; Dorothy Jackson interview, 15 August 1992. **25**: McWhorter, *Yellow Wolf*, 291. **26**: Ibid. **28**: Ibid., 121. **29**: Ibid, 105. **30**: McWhorter, *Hear Me*, 249. **31**: Ibid., 390. **32**: Lynn Pankonin interview, 11 August 1993. **34**: Kevin Peters interview, 19 June 1993; Nancy Halfmoon interview, 15 August 1992. **35**: McWhorter, *Hear Me*, 300-301. **36**: McWhorter Papers, "Peopeo Tholekt's Narrative." **37**: McWhorter, *Yellow Wolf*, 119. **38**: McWhorter, *Hear Me*, 302–3. **39**: Hampton, *Children of Grace*, 167. **40**: Terry Leaf to author, 26 November 1993; Nancy Halfmoon interview, 15 August 1992. **41**: McWhorter, *Yellow Wolf*, 94. **42**: Howard, *Nez Perce Joseph*, 604.